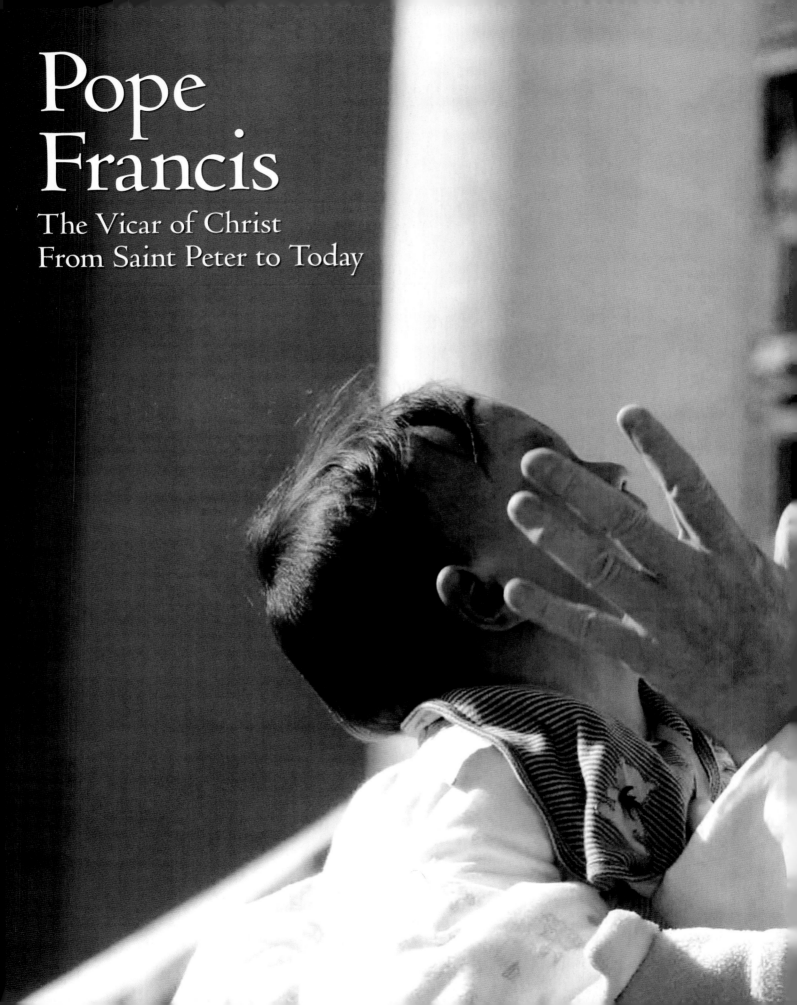

Pope
Francis

The Vicar of Christ
From Saint Peter to Today

LIFE BOOKS
Managing Editor Robert Sullivan
Director of Photography
Barbara Baker Burrows
Creative Director Mimi Park
Deputy Picture Editor Christina Lieberman
Writer-Reporters Michelle DuPré (Chief),
Marilyn Fu, Amy Lennard Goehner, Daniel Levy
Copy Chief Parlan McGaw
Copy Editor Don Armstrong
Photo Associate Sarah Cates
Consulting Picture Editors Mimi Murphy
(Rome), Tala Skari (Paris)
Editorial Director Stephen Koepp

EDITORIAL OPERATIONS
Richard K. Prue (Director), Brian Fellows
(Manager), Richard Shaffer (Production),
Keith Aurelio, Charlotte Coco, Liz Grover, Kevin
Hart, Mert Kerimoglu, Rosalie Khan, Patricia Koh,
Marco Lau, Brian Mai, Po Fung Ng, Rudi Papiri,
Robert Pizaro, Barry Pribula, Clara Renauro,
Katy Saunders, Hia Tan, Vaune Trachtman

TIME HOME ENTERTAINMENT
Publisher Jim Childs
Vice President, Brand & Digital Strategy
Steven Sandonato
Executive Director, Marketing Services
Carol Pittard
Executive Director, Retail & Special Sales
Tom Mifsud
Executive Publishing Director Joy Butts
Director, Bookazine Development & Marketing
Laura Adam
Finance Director Glenn Buonocore
Associate Publishing Director Megan Pearlman
Assistant General Counsel Helen Wan
Assistant Director, Special Sales
Ilene Schreider
Senior Book Production Manager
Susan Chodakiewicz
Design & Prepress Manager
Anne-Michelle Gallero
Brand Manager Roshni Patel
Associate Prepress Manager
Alex Voznesenskiy
Assistant Brand Manager Stephanie Braga

Special thanks: Katherine Barnet,
Jeremy Biloon, Rose Cirrincione,
Jacqueline Fitzgerald, Christine Font,
Jenna Goldberg, Hillary Hirsch, David Kahn,
Amy Mangus, Kimberly Marshall, Amy Migliaccio,
Nina Mistry, Dave Rozzelle, Ricardo Santiago,
Adriana Tierno, Vanessa Wu

ISBN 10: 1-61893-099-0
ISBN 13: 978-1-61893-099-6
Library of Congress Control Number:
2013934624
Vol. 13, No. 8 • March 29, 2013
"LIFE" is a registered trademark of Time Inc.

We welcome your comments and suggestions
about LIFE Books. Please write to us at:
LIFE Books, Attention: Book Editors
PO Box 11016, Des Moines, IA 50336-1016

If you would like to order any of our hardcover
Collector's Edition books, please call us at
1-800-327-6388
(Monday through Friday, 7 a.m.–8 p.m.,
or Saturday, 7 a.m.–6 p.m., Central Time).

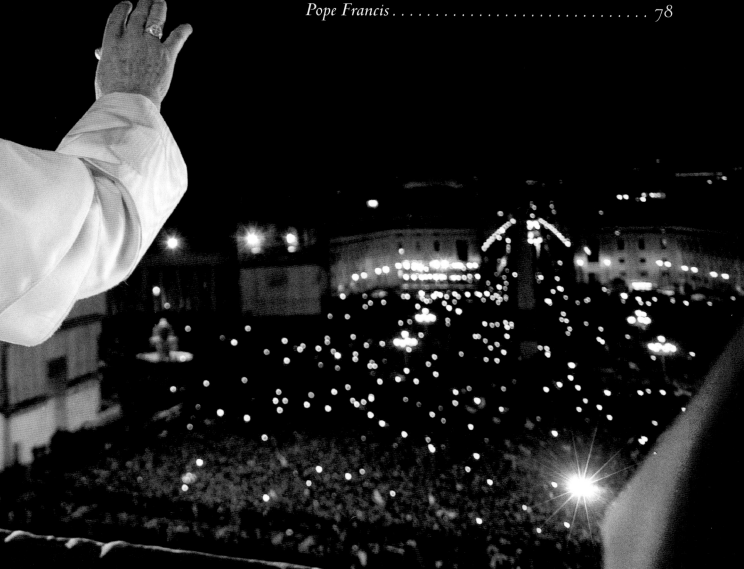

Table of Contents

Front Cover: Pope Francis during his inaugural Mass, March 19, 2013. PHOTOGRAPH BY PAUL HANNA/REUTERS. **Back Cover:** Portrait of Jorge Mario Bergoglio, the future Pope Francis, as a young priest. PHOTOGRAPH FROM PERFIL /SPLASH NEWS. **Page 1:** Pope Francis kneeling in prayer in the Basilica of St. Mary Major in Rome on the day after his election. PHOTOGRAPH FROM L'OSSERVATORE ROMANO/AP.
Pages 2–3: The pope blesses a child as he arrives in St. Peter's Square for his inauguration Mass. PHOTOGRAPH BY CLAUDIO PERI/EPA/LANDOV. **These pages:** Pope Francis waves to the crowd from the central balcony of St. Peter's Basilica after his election on March 13. PHOTOGRAPH FROM SERVIZIOFOTOGRAFICOOR/CPP/POLARIS.

On St. Peter's Throne

Now comes Francis, 266th pope in the line begun by Peter, promising that he and his Church stand ready to serve.

JESUS AND THE EARLY CHRIS-tian evangelists did not necessarily have something called a papacy in mind 2,000 years ago, but they did imagine a Church that would persevere in their time and continue after them. So, yes, when Christ handed the keys of leadership to Peter, he certainly would have hoped that Peter would find a successor, and then there would come another good man, and another. But no human being might have imagined that what has come to be the papal legacy would one day extend to 266 individuals, and that the Church would be so potent still that there is no end in sight. That is the power of Jesus's attraction, and God's promise.

The tremendous excitement that has greeted the coronation of Pope Francis, the former Jorge Mario Cardinal Bergoglio of Argentina, has been wondrous to behold but has tended to obscure some of this long history. All of the news has served to imply that the problems Francis has been called to "deal with" extend about as far back as the first sex-abuse revelation, or the installment of Pope John Paul II in 1978, or maybe to the ancient history of the Vatican II reforms adopted in the 1960s. It is useful—and often fun—to look at the long, dramatic run of the Church, from Peter's day to our own. This is an institution that is as resilient as any, ever, and as adept at weathering storms as Peary or Shackleton. Just to look narrowly at the papacy, as we will in these pages: The men who have sat upon St. Peter's throne have included many saints (literal and not) but also pretenders, poseurs and outright scoundrels. There have been strong popes and weak, brave popes and cowardly, honest popes and dishonest.

In recent history, the Church has had much to be worried about, to be sure, but the great global interest in Francis's election only proves that the Church is still relevant and that people still care. They need their Church, and they need their Church to be good. Refreshingly, Pope Francis has not only admitted but emphasized: The Church needs *them.* In his eloquent and moving homily delivered at St. Peter's during the Mass inaugurating his Petrine ministry on March 19,

he said that on this day "[W]e are celebrating the beginning of the ministry of the new bishop of Rome, the successor of Peter, which also involves a certain power. Certainly, Jesus Christ conferred power upon Peter, but what sort of power was it? Jesus's three questions to Peter about love are followed by three commands: feed my lambs, feed my sheep. Let us never forget that authentic power is service, and that the pope too, when exercising power, must enter ever more fully into that service which has its radiant culmination on the cross. He must be inspired by the lowly, concrete and faithful service that marked Saint Joseph and, like him, he must open his arms to protect all of God's people and embrace with tender affection the whole of humanity, especially the poorest, the weakest, the least important, those whom Matthew lists in the final judgment on love: the hungry, the thirsty, the stranger, the naked, the sick and those in prison. Only those who serve with love are able to protect!"

Christlike words, and certainly directed at today's Church. All of the popes we will meet in these pages had power to a greater or lesser degree. But was it what Francis calls authentic power? *Let us never forget that authentic power is service.*

He has not shrunk, in his first days sitting in the chair, from speaking directly to today's Church leaders, alluding often to what he considers the Church's recent failings. Will he change things? Will he use the Church's still great power to serve, and serve well—thus authenticating his mission and Catholicism's reason for being? He has promised to try.

In the pages that follow are many others who have tried—some giving their lives in the effort—and a few who clearly haven't and have thereby brought shame on their institution. Needless to say, this being LIFE and the Church being the Church, the stories are told not just in narrative but in glorious photography and artwork. Needless to say as well: All of the splendor of Pope Francis's coronation on a brilliant winter's day in Vatican City is our culminating chapter. To look at the pictures, you would think he has triumphed already. As it is, he has asked our blessing for his effort.

Two days after his election, Pope Francis meets with the College of Cardinals in the Clementine Hall of the Apostolic Palace in Vatican City.

Upon This Rock

Jesus gave the keys of His kingdom to the Apostle Peter.
That is where the sometimes wavering line of churchly leaders began.
And now it has led, 265 official popes later, to Francis.

 JESUS OF NAZARETH HAD MANY disciples, 12 of whom—all men—would be elevated by Him and would come to be known as the Apostles. From the scant biographical information in the New Testament it is hard to know their personalities in much depth. Thomas was nervous and skeptical; Judas was nervous and tormented, and in the end he betrayed his leader.

There were two Galilean brothers, sons of John or Jonah, perhaps born in the village of Bethsaida, and both fishermen. They were named Andrew and Peter, also called Simon Peter. It is hard to sketch Andrew. But it is clear that, as Jesus's brief mission among men and women progressed, He saw Peter as a leader: Peter was challenged to follow Jesus onto the waters of the Sea of Galilee; Peter was there on the mountaintop when Jesus was transfigured; Peter was seemingly the most human of the Apostles, faltering in ways familiar to us all (falling asleep when on watch in the Garden of Gethsemane and then, later in the Passion, denying altogether that he even knew Jesus). A friend and, in the biblical narrative, a foil, Peter showed us much about Jesus. Jesus never gave up on Peter. He forgave Peter his human impulses and showed us that God the Father would always do the same. In a crucial episode, he promised Peter the leadership role in this earthly kingdom after His own assignment was finished—he promised Peter, in effect, the first papacy: "And I say unto thee, that thou art Peter, and upon this rock I will build my Church; and the gates of hell shall not prevail against it . . ."—and He never withdrew that pledge. It might be odd to think of it this way, but while they were together during the period of ministry in the Galilee and then Jerusalem, Jesus believed in Peter perhaps more than Peter believed in Him.

After Jesus's crucifixion, there were many disciples who carried the Word, often in clandestine "churches" springing up throughout the Holy Land and gradually spreading toward Rome itself, but among the principals there was Peter, and there was Paul. Jesus's most effective proselytizer, more so even than Peter, did not begin as any kind of follower, and the bare fact that the former Saul of Tarsus

On the opposite page: In St. Peter's Square at the Vatican there is a statue by the 19th century sculptor Giuseppe de Fabris showing the Apostle himself—the man for whom the basilica and plaza are named—holding in his hands the keys given to him by Christ as a symbol of authority among the first Apostles. Fittingly, in the background can be seen a statue of Jesus on the facade of St. Peter's Basilica. At left is Banyas, an antique cave sanctuary of the Greek god Pan. Also known as the Cave of Pan, it is near one of the sources of the Jordan River in the vicinity of Mount Hermon in what was the ancient Roman city of Caesarea Philippi. Jesus and his followers visited this area, where statues of polytheistic gods and nymphs adorned the alcoves of the caves. A strange setting, perhaps, for Jesus to anoint Peter—but maybe not so strange. After all, Jesus's intention was that His Father's Word was to supplant on earth the messages that had been delivered before.

ERICH LESSING/ART RESOURCE, NY

STÉPHANE COMPOINT

became an early Christian evangelist is nothing short of miraculous. Born into a strict Jewish family, Saul was a young Pharisee when he made his way to Jerusalem to study under a renowned rabbi. He was a strong student, and the fervency with which he pursued his Jewish faith knew no bounds. This was in the early years after Jesus's death and, as His story attracted more and more attention, Saul became more fierce in his opposition. He would storm into private houses to seize Jesus-followers and turn them over to jailers, "breathing out threatenings and slaughters against the disciples." So in this period, Saul and Peter, who was establishing the Church in Antioch (then in Syria, now part of Turkey) and presiding for perhaps seven years as leader of the growing Christian community there, were arch enemies. The Jewish high priest was impressed by Saul and gave him permission to go to Damascus, also in Syria, and break up any Jesus cells there. Saul was a thug, and was sent out as a thug. But as Saul came near the city he was blinded by a light, and heard a pleading voice: "Saul, why persecutest thou me? . . . I am Jesus, whom thou persecutest . . . Arise, and go into the city, and it shall be told thee what thou must do." After three days of blindness, Saul was healed, baptized and enlisted in the cause of Christ. He slowly gained credibility with the disciples in Damascus and Jerusalem. Soon to be renamed (and become famous as) Paul, he embarked on his extraordinary mission—to Peter's Antioch, first, and then the port of Seleucia, from which they sailed to Cyprus; to Athens during his second major tour; to Corinth, another thriving port city in what is now southern Greece; to Ephesus, 30 miles south of what is now the Turkish city of Izmir; to Corinth again, to Philippi, Assos, Miletus, Patera; back across the sea (and against the advice of associates) to Jerusalem; finally, as a prisoner, to Rome (with a shipwreck on Malta along the way).

For both Peter and Paul, all roads seemed to lead to Rome, seat of the empire that was determined to crush this bug that was Christianity. As they went, they wrote. The letters of Paul to the various citizenries he was trying to coax and perhaps convert are the greatest interpretations of Jesus's message ever made. Peter is thought to be either the author or the source of the Gospel of Mark, the earliest of the synoptic Gospels in the New Testament and as such, the bedrock of the biographies by Matthew and Luke. Peter's and Paul's words—following Jesus's words—and their courage and their devotion would win the day for Christianity, if persevering against all odds in terrible times can be seen as winning the day. Because of them, there would be a second pope and a third . . . And, eventually, a 266th.

In a painting by the 16th-century Flemish artist Herri met de Bles, we see, in the bottom right, Jesus recruiting the Galilean fisherman Peter to become one of His group of disciples— many of whom, including such famous biblical figures as Mary Magdalene, lived in the region of the Sea of Galilee, which is in fact a large inland lake in Israel. Four of Jesus's Apostles—Andrew, Peter and the brothers John and James—joined Jesus here, and most of His miracles took place here; the Sermon on the Mount was preached nearby. After Jesus commissioned His 12 Apostles during His Galilean ministry, Peter was always by His side, and was rewarded for it, as recorded by Mark (who may have been Peter himself, but if not was a disciple and mouthpiece): "Now Jesus and his disciples went out to the town of Caesarea Philippi; and on the road he asked his disciples, saying to them, 'Who do men say that I am?'" And Simon Peter confessed Jesus to be the "Son of the living God," whereupon, by tradition, Jesus "handed the keys" to Peter— designating him as "this rock" upon which Christianity would be built.

SCALA/ART RESOURCE, NY

ERICH LESSING/ART RESOURCE, NY

The altarpiece detail at top left shows the regard in which Saint Paul was held by later generations of his Church; among those who continued Jesus's work after His death, Paul was the most influential, growing famous even in his own day. At left is the Via Egnatia near Philippi; Paul visited the city three times in the years circa 49 to 57, helping make it one of the early Christian strongholds in Greece, and his Epistle to the Philippians remains one of history's great rhapsodies on the themes of love and

peace. Above is the theater in Ephesus, which could hold up to 25,000 people; Paul preached here circa A.D. 57. Paul went to Ephesus, 30 miles from what is now the Turkish city of Izmir, twice, stopping briefly here near the end of his second missionary journey, then spending more than two years here during his third and final mission. What happened the latter time says a lot about Ephesus and about the success Paul was having. The old town was still invested in the fertility goddess Artemis when Paul first visited, and local craftsmen saw their brisk trade in replicas and souvenirs for pilgrims threatened by Christianity's rise. They denounced Paul and staged an anti-Christian riot. Paul moved on from Ephesus dejected. But when he returned he was welcomed, heralded.

Times and attitudes had— very quickly—changed, no small thanks to Paul himself and his message. As Professor Shaye J.D. Cohen of Harvard has observed, "The wondrous thing about Jesus is not that He was believed to possess such power that He attracted followers. The wondrous thing about it is that even after He was executed for being a troublemaker, His followers did not disappear. They did not just go away. Somehow, His death proved to be the catalyst for the emergence of something very new and very different."

13

"And I will give unto thee the keys of the kingdom of heaven: and whatsoever thou shalt bind on earth shall be bound in heaven; and whatever thou shalt loose on earth shall be loosed in heaven." What Jesus did not presage for Peter was that the Church would be built in Rome, that "this rock" would be in the very place where the emperor's awesome earthly empire was then headquartered.

We are told what delivered Paul to Rome: an arrest for agitating in Jerusalem, and his demand that as a Roman citizen he was due a trial in the capital. But as with the case of Peter, there are no biblical accounts of his fate in that city—nothing about where either of them lived, what they might have done there. Early Christian evidence indicates that they went there, and eventually traditions of Peter joining Paul in Roman

martyrdom became part of the narrative. But we can't be sure. What we can know is only that Paul traveled widely and evangelized, while Peter had a career as a leading Jesus disciple in the Holy Land. In that role, he was influential in endorsing Paul's opinion that Gentiles, too, should be recruited—not just Judaean Jews. He wanted an inclusive Church, one that might grow large.

These opinions, jointly held and espoused more forcefully and publicly over time, would have put both men in opposition to the emperor. And who would that emperor have been, in the years when Peter and Paul were active?

The last three rulers of Rome's Julio-Claudian dynasty are all famous: the notorious Caligula, who was assassinated in A.D. 41; Caligula's uncle Claudius, who ruled until his death

in 54; and Nero, stepson of Claudius, who was in charge from 54 until becoming the first Roman emperor to commit suicide, in the year 68. It was this last man who is associated by tradition with the persecution and deaths of Peter and Paul. He is seen as a young man in the statue at left, which is in the Gregorian Profane Museum in Vatican City, and opposite is the giant Egyptian obelisk imported to Rome by Caligula, which decorated Nero's infamous circus: an arena where, among other events, Christians were put to death. The obelisk had already become part of the Vatican piazza when this stereoscopic image was made in the 19th century, and since it remains in place, it will be an oft-recurring image— an anchor of sorts—in these pages.

At left, bottom, is the disputation between Peter, Paul and Simon Magus in the presence of Emperor Nero. This incident surely never took place. Simon was a Samaritan sorcerer and converted Christian who had a following in Rome, and was confronted by Peter for his practice of selling ecclesiastical preferences (a practice known down the centuries as "simony"). According to the apocryphal narrative called Acts of Peter and Paul, Nero is mediating a debate among the three men and at one point Simon levitates (as he reputedly could do at will) but then suffers a fall and is killed. Peter and Paul are subsequently imprisoned.

The Acts of Peter and Paul is one of a proliferation of nonbiblical documents that were written over many decades after Christ's death, and led eventually to accepted lore, or even what is called religious tradition. The tradition accepted by many is that Peter and Paul were put to death by Nero.

The death of the first pope: Whence Peter came is recounted in the New Testament, largely in the Acts of the Apostles; whither he went and where he was buried are parts of apocryphal tradition. At left is David's Tower and the Old City wall seen through an olive grove on the Israeli side of Jerusalem in 1957, looking much as it might have looked when Peter, after Christ's ascension, bravely started defending his late mentor in front of Jewish scribes and laypeople. It might have all ended here for Peter; we cannot know for certain (and in fact there have long been rumors that he was buried in a Christian cemetery in Jerusalem). But over the first two to three centuries following Jesus's death, the common narrative placed Peter in Rome alongside Paul. Historians, including Tacitus, as well as Christian theologians, wrote of Nero's persecution of Christians, and by the 2nd century there were reports in apocryphal accounts of an Apostle having been a victim of the violence. Other histories have Paul surviving Rome and traveling on, and Peter's episcopate in the city lasting 25 years. But Eusebius, writing in the early 4th century, says Paul was killed in Nero's Christian bloodbath—beheaded, according to the chronicler— and in this somewhat later period the account wherein Peter and Paul are both crucified by the emperor has gained currency. In the account that survives most durably, modest Peter asks that he be allowed to die on an inverted cross, feeling himself unworthy to be executed upright, as was Christ. Below: a 15th-century French depiction, "Crucifixion of Saint Peter with a Donor."

The early Christian Church, still under assault throughout the Roman Empire during the 2nd, 3rd and early 4th centuries, saw in the examples of heroic Peter and Paul an inspiration to soldier on—and often to give all, including life itself—in the name of Christ. This is the astonishing thing about Christianity, as Harvard's Professor Cohen observed earlier: its durability, its perseverance. Certainly this is a testament to the attractive and singular philosophy of Christ, which was unique in its day, even radical or insurrectionist. The idea of giving a cloak to one's brother or turning the other cheek in that violent age seemed crazy to many in authority, appealing to the downtrodden. The survival of Christianity is also, of course, a testament to the earliest, most dogged and devout Christians.

There was a terrible symbiotic relationship between the Roman Empire and the early Christian churches: a willingness to martyr, and a willingness to be martyred. Before Christianity was legalized with the Edict of Milan, which we will learn more about in our subsequent chapter on Constantine the Great, Christians could be and would be persecuted on an ad hoc basis. Nothing was required to put a targeted individual on trial other than a prosecutor, a charge of Christianity and a local official willing to mete out punishment after a pro forma conviction. In the vast empire, where local governance was the rule, there were more than enough governors willing to play their roles. In the photograph at top, left, that is indeed a Roman amphitheater—but it's not in Rome. Dating to the 2nd century, it is in Tarragona, in the Catalonia region of Spain.

It was the site of early Christian martyrdoms. Victims could be crucified, burned, stoned, beheaded, impaled or, yes, forced to do battle with animals, including lions. (Opposite, bottom: Varieties of capital punishment facing the early Christians, as depicted in a 16th-century fresco.) What developed in this period was a sense among Christians of the ultimate glory of martyrdom. It was Christ-like to witness and to be killed, was it not? Peter and Paul had, as far as the Christians knew, been martyred by Nero. This would be the direct route to heaven—to the warmth and comfort of Jesus and God the Father. Martyrdom was considered "baptism in blood," and martyrs were seen as intercessors—one foot in either kingdom.

Church leaders saw, quite rightly, that a movement under siege could hardly afford to lose its troops in great numbers, and looked to scripture to convince followers that willful martyrdom—shouting "I am a Christian!" from the mountaintops—was not the same thing as what Jesus had experienced, and could be considered akin to suicide, which was a sin. As was pointed out by theologians: Jesus had urged in the Gospel of Matthew, "When they persecute you in one town, flee to the next," and in the book of Acts there were accounts of the earliest clandestine churches constantly moving about to avoid the authorities. (Above is a warren of caves in Cappadocia, Turkey, where Christian worshippers once operated in secret.) It took time, but the Christian attitude evolved from thinking of martyrdom as a quick route out of a miserable existence on earth to a divine one in Paradise to: Stand and be counted. Stand and fight.

19

SEPULCRUM
SANCTI PETRI APOSTOLI

Peter lives! First, most importantly, he lives on in a line of 266 popes and the continued relevance of his Church after nearly two millennia. In physical manifestations, there are thousands of cathedrals and chapels dedicated to him around the globe, including, it is interesting to note, one in Jerusalem. Other things: In the photograph at left, top, is Peter's Cathedra, or throne, as encased in gilded bronze and designed by Gian Lorenzo Bernini, the great artist who worked on many embellishments of the Vatican in the 1600s. At left, bottom, is Peter's tomb, also in—or, rather, below—St. Peter's Basilica (and then there's the basilica itself, as the world's greatest memorial to Peter). To return to where our chapter began: There is, above, the sculpture in the plaza by Giuseppe de Fabris, seemingly being acknowledged by Peter's

most recent successor, Francis, during the new pope's first appearance before his people on March 13, 2013.

It's interesting to look back at this man, Peter, whom we now see as the inaugural pope, but who lived in a time when there was no papacy. The Bible implies that he was married, so a couple of now-emphatic traditions were broken before they were established. He was sometimes weak. He was, according to Luke's gospel, sometimes at odds with his fellow Apostles, who were doubtful about granting him primacy.

But as with so many things in the life of Jesus, from the first tentative steps of His ministry to His world-altering death, Christ must have been right in His choice of Peter. There is little question but that the Apostle grew in his role once he was forced to carry on without his leader. If we contrast the Peter who denied Jesus thrice before cockcrow with the chastened, strengthened Peter who started preaching the Word in the Holy Land soon after Christ's crucifixion, we have to wonder if we are dealing with the same man. Most probably, we are seeing a changed man.

There was no way Christ in human form, or Peter or Paul, was going to witness the glory of their temporal Church. It simply couldn't happen that fast. But when you think about it: three centuries of growth in the face of—in the teeth of—an opponent so awesome as the Roman Empire, and then liberation . . . All of this in a time when affairs perforce could not move rapidly . . .

Well, it seems the rise of Christianity was pretty fast after all.

If it needed a transcendent and preternaturally wise figure—Jesus—to launch it and give it spiritual bedrock forevermore, it needed mere mortals to move it forward. Peter played his part, and so did Paul. Thousands of individuals, men and women, many of whom you will meet in the pages ahead, played theirs.

And now, Pope Francis begins his ultimate chapter in the Church, certainly looking to Peter for that special strength that sometimes accrues to one who is chosen.

Constantine the Great

At right is a mosaic in the Byzantine Church of the Holy Savior in Chora, which is located in Istanbul, the city in Turkey that was, of course, once called Constantinople in honor of the man depicted here. At far right is a fresco in the Room of Constantine, one of the four 16th-century Stanze di Raffaello (Raphael's Rooms) in the Vatican. In the central scene is the so-called Vision of the Cross, which is a central element (along with his mother's influence, to be discussed on the next pages) in the emperor's drift toward Christianity. What had happened: On May 1, 305, Diocletian and his co-emperor stepped down as overarching rulers of Rome and their deputy Caesars, including Maximinus and Constantius, Constantine's father, started squabbling for control. Constantius died in 306 and his former troops chose to stand with Constantine, who, after a time of avoiding conflict with Maxentius, Maximinus's son, decided to push the battle in the spring of 312. As the year progressed, Constantine won the day in Turin and Verona and came to control northern Italy, then, in October, with his army poised to engage Maxentius's main brigades at the strategically crucial Milvian Bridge on the Tiber, Constantine had his vision. Accounts vary, but the gist is (and the chronicler Eusebius says he got it from the emperor himself): Constantine looked up at one point, perhaps into the sun, and saw a cross made of light, and with it a promise and an urging—"Through this sign you will conquer." During a dream following the vision, Constantine came to understand that if he fought in the name of Christ, using the

RICHARD T. NOWITZ/CORBIS

True Cross as his emblem in battle, he would prevail. He did win at Milvian Bridge, Maxentius was drowned in the Tiber, Constantine marched on to become the sole ruler of the empire, and Christian symbolism was emblazoned on all his men's shields. Constantine did not personally convert to Christianity at this point, but he obviously came to feel well disposed toward a movement that was, with or without him, on the rise in Rome.

IN THIS BOOK CELEBRATING the investiture of Pope Francis and reviewing the history of the papacy, Constantine, never a pope nor even a priest, is an anomaly. Why, then, is he in these pages at all? The answer is that, without him, Pope Francis and the lineage of all others from the 4th century onward might not have been possible. Constantine was Christianity's great enabler, the bridge that was needed between Jesus, Peter, Paul and the many other martyrs—the bridge to everything that would follow once the Roman Empire set out on a path to becoming a Christian state, breeding ground

CORBIS

He wasn't a disciple, he wasn't a pope, he wasn't a cardinal or a bishop or a priest. For all but the briefest time, he wasn't even a Christian. But he was a Roman emperor, so when he converted at last, the Western world was turned upside down.

of the several Christian religions we know today.

That certainly never could have been predicted. Flavius Valerius Constantinus was born in what is now Serbia circa 280 to an officer in the Roman army and a woman of low birth who may have been his father's concubine. That father did well and was named governor of Dalmatia by Emperor Diocletian: the family's first substantial link with a very volatile man. Beginning in 286, Diocletian would divide his empire and then create junior emperors in various regions; one of his first trusted "Caesars" was Constantine's father. Living in the court of Diocletian, Constantine himself was primed for greatness; he was schooled and trained and eventually given advancement.

He was present for the outset of Diocletian's Great Persecution, the worst-yet campaign to eradicate Christianity from Rome and the empire. Churches were sacked and burned; holdings were stolen; thousands of people were killed. Constantine later claimed he had nothing to do with the Persecution. History indicates that he did nothing to stop it. As we see in this chapter, something (a political or religious epiphany?) delivered him to a point where he acted decisively—decisively indeed, and with vast consequence.

One way of looking at it is that, with teachings so strong and the bare fact that He was the Son of God, Jesus was simply not to be denied, and the Christian movement would be unstoppable because of Him, despite the efforts of Nero, Diocletian and all the others. Another—and not entirely secular or irreligious view—is that the success of Christianity would have been impossible if not for the dedicated actions of several who came after Christ. Without the narratives of the Gospel writers Mark, Matthew, Luke and John (and others not included in the canonical New Testament); without the feverish evangelization of Saint Paul; without the devotion and example of the first martyred pope—without each of these, Christianity faced a more difficult road. Without any of them, it might have faced an impossible one.

Could the religion have been stopped by the continued persecution of Roman emperors? We will never know, because Constantine had his vision—and his mom. Not only the son, but the mother, Helena, seen below, left, in a depiction from the altarpiece of Santa Cruz de Bleza, is today regarded as a saint by many Christian faiths. Empress Helena, who as we already know was herself lowly born, was said to have worked among the poor and released many prisoners, perhaps setting an example for her son of what would become known in later ages as "Christian charity." She is even better remembered for finding fragments of the True Cross upon which Jesus was crucified, and this reputation in her day may have influenced the various readings of Constantine's dream.

The extraordinary hallway below is the nave of the Basilica of St. John Lateran in Rome, an adjunct of the Lateran Palace, which came into Constantine's possession after his triumph at Milvian Bridge.

St. John Lateran is the oldest and highest ranked of the four Papal Basilicas in the Italian capital, located just outside the formal boundaries of Vatican City, and is the most famous home of popes except for the Vatican itself. There used to be a fort on the site, but after Constantine defeated Maxentius at the bridge, the fort was torn down and an administration building was established. Constantine gave the place to the bishop

THE ART ARCHIVE/CORBIS

ALINARI/ART RESOURCE, NY

of Rome shortly thereafter (perhaps his greatest gift to the Church this side of his allowance of freedom of religion), and it became the headquarters of Pope Sylvester I (he dedicated the Basilica and Lateran Palace in 1324). At the entrance are these words: "Most Holy Lateran Church, of all the churches in the city and the world, the mother and head."

Briefly alluded to above is the gift of "freedom of religion" in Rome: This references the Edict of Milan of 313, and it is more important here than the Battle of Milvian Bridge or even Constantine's deathbed conversion.

It certainly can be argued that Constantine, who would become above all the first Christian emperor of Rome, saw the writing on the wall, and assumed that Christianity, extraordinarily resilient as it was proving to be even in the face of the most vicious persecutions of Roman authority, represented the future—a stronger, more stable future. This view becomes more attractive when we look closely at the résumé of Constantine the man, who was not attractive in character but as ruthless as any who had preceded him on the throne: a fierce fighter, a horrible father and husband (at one point he had his wife and son executed for reasons unknown). He doesn't seem, on the page, a model Christian. And yet one of his earliest rulings, the Edict of Milan, changed Christianity from an illicit faith into a legal one, to be treated "with benevolence." He never did make Christ-worship the official state religion of Rome, but with his church-building and other encouragements, he all but did so. Certainly the Church was pleased with the gifts of mortar and spirit, and, initially, was much pleased with the emperor. At right, we see the pope blessing Constantine.

On these pages, two pictures of and from the Hagia Sophia, once one of the world's great Christian cathedrals, in Constantinople, today a fantastic museum, in the renamed Istanbul. At left is an aerial view with the Bosporus Strait in the distance, and in the 10th century mosaic above we have Emperor Justinian (483–565) offering the Hagia Sophia, and Emperor Constantine offering his city of Constantinople to the Virgin Mary and the Christ child.

What's all this about? Who's Justinian? How did we get to Turkey?

We must remember that Constantine was a political leader, not a pope, and whatever sentimentality he might have felt for the city where Peter and Paul were said to have been martyred was slight. He eventually sought to shift the nucleus of his expansive operation from Rome to what he considered a more central location, and his pick was the ancient town of Byzantium. It was rechristened Constantinople in 330 and in short order grew to rival Rome itself

in political, economic and Christian influence. Constantine died in 337, having converted on his deathbed to the religion he had helped to build up.

Within decades it became clear that the Byzantine (as it would be called) was a whole new empire, free of many old influences and eager to blend parts of the local cultural heritage with what its first emperor had brought from Italy. The formal split of the Roman Empire occurred in 395. Already the Constantinople-led Eastern half was flourishing, and would continue to do so. The Western half, based in Rome, would struggle for a time and then would come to be controlled completely by the Church, and would rise again. That half is our concern in the remainder of our book.

But before we leave Constantine and Constantinople: In the 6th century, at its greatest reach geographically, the Byzantine Empire's footprint encircled the Mediterranean Sea, from Italy and the Balkans to Asia Minor, the Middle East, North Africa and southern

Spain. (To answer an earlier question: Justinian the Great was Byzantine emperor from 527 to 565.) The Eastern Empire had, from the first, exhibited resistance to any imposition of language or culture by the Western Empire—to Latinization— and had clung to its Greek roots. If you perceive this leading, in the Christian strain, to Greek Orthodoxy, you are correct. Byzantine emperors were considered to be handpicked by God, and the affairs of state they oversaw often were concerned with preservation of Orthodox ("right believing") Christianity. Predictably, that led to dustups between Rome and Constantinople's top bishop, a position in Christendom that was second only to the pope's.

But that's a whole other book. We have to turn now from the awe-inspiring 6th-century Hagia Sophia to the story of another great edifice—another great complex—the Vatican, where the Church that would welcome its first Pope Francis in 2013 would grow to a glorious immensity.

The Vatican Through the Years

VATICAN HILL IS, IN LATIN, *Mons Vaticanus*, and that's what all this was, way back when: a piece of earth slightly elevated from what was called Vatican Fields. Today, Michelangelo's masterwork St. Peter's Basilica (seen here in the distance), the Apostolic Palace, the Sistine Chapel and all the Vatican Museums dominate Mons Vaticanus. Consider just the museums: In a Roman vineyard in 1506, at which point the Vatican had been planned and was being executed, a monumental statue of Laocoön, a great priest in Greek mythology, was discovered near where the emperor Nero once lived. Pope Julius II heard of the find and sent two artists who were working at the Vatican to examine the statue. One of these artists was Michelangelo Buonarotti—and of course this chapter of our book will largely belong to him. They reported to the pope that it was a masterpiece and that he should buy it from the vineyard owner. He did, and thus the Vatican Museums were born. Today, the artistic holdings of the Roman Catholic Church are among the world's most extensive and fabulous and are on display in dozens of galleries in various museums within Vatican City. The Vatican Library, which includes the Sistine Hall, contains not only manuscripts but hundreds of thousands of medals, coins, prints and engravings as well. Items from ancient Egypt, including the Book of the Dead, are housed in the Museo Egizio. In the Museo Pio-Clementino, there are 53 galleries of Greek and Roman sculpture to pass through before arriving at the transcendental Sistine Chapel, where only days ago the College of Cardinals gathered and elected Jorge Cardinal Bergoglio as their pope.

Mons Vaticanus, on the west bank of the Tiber River, has always been a little separate from the city of Rome and has long been protected by popes as their domain—ever since Leo IV in the 9th century. But in our pages we seek more than just-the-facts answers; we want to comprehend this place where the Church has grown to such magnificence as described above in just a few of its holdings, and as represented by a flock of 1.2 billion. An American might understand the Vatican as the Catholic White House. But it is so much older—and the Church is so much older than our democracy—and what it has represented at twists and turns in the story explains much, and adds to our appreciation of Francis's Church.

As mentioned, the building that you espy, lit up in the nighttime at right in a view from nearby Castel Sant'Angelo, is the Papal Basilica of St. Peter in the Vatican, and for many it is the Vatican, which is okay. It is certainly the most famous work of Renaissance architecture in the world, and is the center not only of Vatican City but of the Roman Catholic Church. Having said that, it is not the so-called mother church— St. John Lateran retains that distinction—nor the home cathedral of the bishop of Rome (again, St. John Lateran). It is said to sit atop the tomb of Saint Peter (and as we will shortly see, there is some evidence that this is true), and a host of other popes are buried in its many grave sites. It is one of the very largest churches in the world and is the hub not only of a local congregation but a global enterprise. As a city-state, the Vatican is tiny; as a religious edifice or commune, it is sprawling and incomprehensibly grand. The basilica and adjacent buildings rival Machu Picchu and Angkor Wat in transcendence, inscrutability and a sheer sense of marvelousness. The interesting thing, as we begin to tour the Vatican, is this: If Christianity is essentially two millennia old, the movement traveled the first three quarters of its history without this place. That's when the going was toughest. Once the Church was bold enough to lay the cornerstone of St. Peter's Basilica, there would be no stopping it.

A building, a city, a state: these days a place of joy as Francis begins his pontificate. The Vatican's history is complicated, but to many, it is a man in a window, a throng in the plaza below and a once-in-a-lifetime blessing.

Above is an engraving of the so-called seven churches of Rome when Christianity was asserting itself, mightily, in all precincts; that's the Tiber River bisecting the city. At right, located in the oldest part of the Vatican Gardens, is the Villa Pia, which now houses the headquarters of the Pontifical Academy of Social Sciences. This building has served as a summer residence of the pope, and back when this sector was still rich with game it was a hunting lodge. The setting here clearly could not be more idyllic, with four elaborately decorated buildings surrounding a courtyard paved with a marble ellipse, and in the background: the dome of St. Peter's Basilica. Is there a loftier place on earth? From the outset, the Vatican was meant to be splendid, and the gardens, which cover 57 acres (most of Vatican Hill) and account for more than half of all territory within Vatican City, have long been considered attractions of near equal beauty to the cathedrals and chapels. They started as orchards and vineyards in back of the Apostolic Palace in the Middle Ages; Nicholas II planted a lawn, garden and orchard in the 13th century. The gardens were firmly established during the Renaissance and Baroque periods, when fountains, sculptures and all manner of imported vegetation were added. The Church was now mighty, and certainly never shrank from sacking other European nations or, really, anywhere at all. Much of the plunder of the Crusades was now deployed throughout the Vatican, and major artworks were donated—or otherwise found their way—to the Church in Rome. The Vatican's opulence has always been one its true delights, and also a source of considerable criticism. Christ spoke for the poor (as Francis now does). The Vatican glories in Christ, but there's nothing poor about it.

31

a 30-year-old sculptor who had been in and out of Rome for about a decade but seemed to prefer Florence. (Actually, we know that he preferred it. When he died at the height of his prominence, in 1564, after a remarkable 88-year life, his body, by his prearrangement, was snuck out of Rome to be buried in Florence.)

But anyway, before he turned 30 he had already created his "David" and "Pietà," the latter of which was praised by the contemporaneous artist and writer Giorgio Vasari as "a revelation of all the potentialities and force of the art of sculpture. It is certainly a miracle that a formless block of stone could ever have been reduced to a perfection that nature is scarcely able to create in the flesh." Michelangelo had made the "Pietà," which resides (and will forevermore) in St. Peter's Basilica, when he was 24, and now, in 1505, Pope Julius II summoned him back to Rome for an even bigger job: his (Julius's) tomb. But funding for the project was uncertain, and Michelangelo kept getting thrown new commissions, by Julius and others, and the tomb wouldn't be finished for 40 years (and even then, not to Michelangelo's satisfaction). In the interim, all those other commissions and creations . . . Well, what can you say

The Vatican was not designed solely by the sculptor, painter and architect Michelangelo di Lodovico Buonarroti Simoni—not solely, not hardly. It was designed principally by Donato Bramante, Carlo Maderno, Gian Lorenzo Bernini, Antonio da Sangallo the Younger—and Michelangelo. In the space we have available here, we will dwell on Michelangelo.

Its location was preordained by history. At the time of Christ, Agrippina the Elder drained this sector across the Tiber from the city and planted her gardens. Not long after, Emperor Caligula ordered a circus, or amphitheater, built upon the site—he had the original Vatican obelisk brought in from Heliopolis in Egypt—and this was completed in the 1st century by Nero, who loved the circus only too well. After the Great Fire of Rome in the year 64, many Christians were killed here; it could be that Saint Peter was crucified right here. It was already a place of life and death and Christian involvement when, in 326, a Constantinian basilica became the first church to rise on this already hallowed spot. Construction of the present St. Peter's Basilica began on April 18, 1506, and would continue for 120 years.

In 1506, Michelangelo was

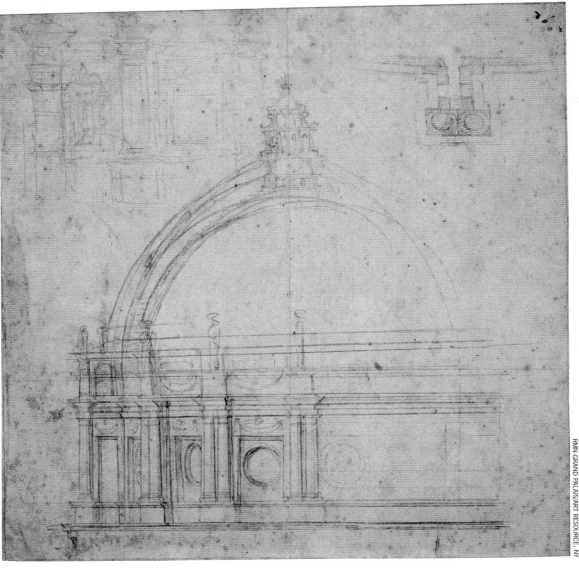

beyond, perhaps, Holy Moses!

From 1508 to 1512 he painted the ceiling of the Sistine Chapel, and we will discuss this in more detail a few pages on. What we see on these two pages: sketches for the building of the basilica and its dome, the latter commission assumed from Antonio da Sangallo the Younger and not quite finished in Michelangelo's lifetime, but reflecting his genius top to bottom. The dome itself, with its double shell, has an inside diameter of half a football field, an interior height of a hundred yards and a height to the top of the cross of nearly 150 yards. It is lighted, brilliantly, by 16 windows. On the perimeter is the inscription,

"You are Peter and upon this rock I will build my church and I'll give you the keys of the kingdom of heaven." The dome would be the model for subsequent architectural achievements throughout the world such as St. Paul's Cathedral in London, which was completed in 1710; the Invalides in Paris, built between 1671 and 1676; and our own U.S. Capitol, which rose on a hilltop in Washington, D.C., beginning in 1793. On the pages following: Michelangelo's last great murals in Rome are on the sidewalls of the private Pauline Chapel in the Apostolic Palace. This room is also known as the private papal chapel, or the pope's prayer space.

Before we return to the utter beauty of Michelangelo's work, a brief tour of the semisecret Vatican: the vaults and netherworld that represent so much of the Church's history. Above is the Vatican grotto and on the opposite page, clockwise from top left, we have the tomb of Pope Boniface VIII, one of several papal burial sites underneath the Vatican; the excavation of St. Peter's Church, which was an exciting enterprise indeed; and the stone sarcophagus of Pope Pius XI in the upper grottoes. The tradition always

was that Saint Peter had been martyred on this spot, but proof was unavailable for centuries (not that it was needed by the faithful). Today there is a site under St. Peter's Basilica called St. Peter's tomb—a few graves and some remnants of a structure that, claims the Vatican, was built to commemorate Peter's place of death. Certainly the mausoleums here are old, dating to the 2nd, 3rd and early 4th centuries, and there is solid evidence that this place was once filled in as part of the foundation of the original St. Peter's,

built in the 4th century, when Constantine I was in charge. An excavation in the first half of the 20th century turned up many bones—of humans and animals— but none that could be conclusively tied to Peter. A subsequent examination found not only more bones but an inscription regarding a "Petrus." On June 26, 1968, Pope Paul VI proclaimed, not to universal acceptance, that Peter's burial place had been found. Looked at one way: It really doesn't matter. Peter certainly lived and died, and he set Christ's Church

on the path that would lead, in 2013, to Francis. But for all the same reasons that people travel to the Vatican in order to further their devotion to God and Christ, they care that Peter is buried there—and this is fine. The grave said by the Church to be that of the first pope was found to contain the bones of, among others, a 60- to 70-year-old man. One argument is that Peter's remains were found during the time of Constantine and placed here, another is that we can't possibly know whose bones these were and to

whom the inscription refers. The Vatican lives on, so does the Church, so does Peter. As for Boniface VIII and Pius XI: The former had a decade-long term as pope at the end of the 13th century and is remembered today for his feuds with Dante, who placed him in the eighth circle of Hell in The Divine Comedy; the latter served from 1922 to 1939 and leaves a legacy of having been strongly antifascist between the two world wars, and having encouraged a greater involvement in the Church by lay Catholics.

This is the room that all Catholics and millions more people hope to visit one day, and it can be reliably reported: The Sistine Chapel is perhaps smaller than you might think, but a thousand-fold more grand than ordinary imagination can conceive. It belongs to the Church and also, of course, to Michelangelo. His associate and rival Raphael was working at the Vatican at the same time in the early 1500s, and was at the peak of his powers, but this big assignment fell to Michelangelo, who didn't yet have Raphael's reputation for either painting or for frescoes, but who was game and ambitious. He oversaw the establishment of the scaffolding, he hoisted himself up and he got to work—work that would take approximately four years (but when the result is considered, that seems like no time).

The project was Pope Julius II's idea, but once Michelangelo was on the job, Julius's original thoughts were scrapped and inspiration took over; a (relatively) simple plan became a sweeping history of the Bible with more than 300 figures painted on a surface area of more than a thousand square yards. Everything from the "Drunkenness of Noah" to "God Creating the Sun and the Moon" to the "Garden of Eden" would be part of this astonishing effort. It's interesting: Michelangelo's own religious impulses were as a seeker and often a doubter. Not only wasn't he rapturously devout, he wasn't particularly sociable. In short, he wouldn't have been seen as any kind of religious or human charismatic figure. But when he lost himself in his work, he was somehow transformed. Perhaps more simply: His talent was unleashed.

He knew what he wanted to do, he always knew what he wanted to do, and once he got going with the Sistine Chapel, he developed a firm vision. At one point, Pope Julius asked the artist to retouch some figures in gold so the depicted people wouldn't look so poor. Michelangelo replied that these subjects had most likely been very poor when on earth, and that was the end of the discussion. Similarly, the original commission called for the 12 Apostles against a star-filled sky. Michelangelo instead saw something altogether more elaborate: a section on the Fall of Man, and then the prophets' Promise of Salvation, and also a Genealogy of Christ. This, of course, is what now adorns the chapel ceiling, including the "Creation of Adam," "Creation of Eve," "Deluge," "Isaiah," "Cumaean Sibyl" and more. The nice starry-sky picture remains to be painted elsewhere by someone else.

In the pictures at right we see two details of the ceiling, the top one illustrating how much dirt and grime accrued over the centuries, and the bottom after a cleaning and restoration in the 1980s and '90s. Opposite: On January 22, 2006, the Vatican's Secretary of State Angelo Sodano, presides at a Mass for the 110 members of the Swiss Guard. The Italian Sodano remains, at 85 years of age in 2013, the dean of the Vatican's College of Cardinals.

St. Peter's Square, then and now: In the stereoscopic card detail from the 19th century, the Egyptian obelisk is an identifying figure, as it is today, but the grand approach that we now know is choked with buildings. None other than the fascist dictator Benito Mussolini ordered the destruction of the buildings—he presided with customary fervor and showmanship at the first pickax blow in 1936—and the construction of the broad entrance avenue. At right we see the pilgrims gathered on Wednesday, March 13, 2013, on which day they will learn of their new pope, Francis, the former Jorge Mario Cardinal Bergoglio of Argentina. Neither wind nor rain has ever deterred the faithful from filling the immense plaza of St. Peter's for important greetings or farewells, holiday season Masses or just regularly scheduled blessings from the papal balcony. The square was designed by Gian Lorenzo Bernini and built between 1656 and 1667. At the center is the obelisk dating from the 13th century B.C., which, as mentioned earlier in our book, was brought to Rome in the 1st century A.D. by Caligula to adorn the circus that he developed and Nero completed. Many Christians were sacrificed in the Roman arena where the obelisk once stood—on a spot just to the south of today's basilica, close to the present sacristy. Pope Sixtus V had Domenico Fontana move the obelisk to the center of St. Peter's Square in 1586. A last note: The obelisk is a symbol of whence the Church has come, and it is also a functioning sun dial; its shadow marks noon over zodiac signs inlaid in white marble paving stones within the square. Almost certainly, no other icon associated with Catholicism brings into play polytheistic Ancient Egypt, the virulently anti-Christian Roman Empire and astrology as represented by the zodiac. But there it is, and there it stands.

The Papacy Through the Years

AS INTRIGUING AS THE FOUND-ing and subsequent history of the Vatican was and is, it is as nothing compared to the intrigues behind not-always-closed Vatican doors: the rather astonishing history of the men (and women) who have walked those halls, led this Church and left behind legacies that will be forever debated. One person's good pope is another's bad, there were women working behind the scenes—it's all better than Dan Brown. You doubt? Read on.

In walking through this narrative, we will try to highlight issues—and people—that may be seen as pertinent to the discussions of the last few weeks leading up to the conclave that chose Pope Francis. For instance, everyone was wondering whether the new pope would be Italian, noting that the last two (the German Benedict XVI and the Polish John Paul II) were not. Many seemed to think that everyone subsequent to the Galilean fisherman Peter was from Rome or environs. Not true, not at all. It certainly was the case that, before Karol Wojtyla was chosen to succeed John Paul I in 1978 (the "Year of Three Popes"), the Italian string extended all the way back to Adrian VI in the 16th century; but strings are made to be broken. And besides, before Adrian there had been many non-Italians: 14 French, 11 Greek, six German, six Syrian, three African, three Spanish, one Dutch, one English and one Portuguese (these categorized with the caveat that they fit today's political definitions; an early pope described as Greek may have been born in a Greek colony on the Italian peninsula). Adrian VI, a Flemish ship carpenter's son born Adrian Florenszoon Boeyens, was such an unpopular man, he perhaps encouraged thinking among the Italian bloc: no more foreigners. He was a tutor to the Spanish emperor Charles V and was for a period Grand Inquisitor. His papacy was anathema to hedonistic Romans. His meals were prepared by an old Flemish retainer, and the papal laundry, so the gossip went, was hung to dry in the papal apartments. When his reign ended after just 21 months, in 1523, garlands of flowers were sent to the doctor at whose hands he had died.

Earlier non-Italian popes were generally better regarded, but some—particularly the Borgia pope Alexander VI—not much. Victor I, whose term was from 189 to 198, was the first of the three African-born bishops of Rome. He is remembered as the pope who insisted that Easter be celebrated on Sunday rather than on Passover, which might fall anywhere in the week. When certain churches in Asia Minor chose to ignore the Roman bishop's edict, Victor excommunicated them. The gesture is an early example of the prerogatives Rome claimed for itself (see how the Curia thinks today that the Vatican Bank is somehow a bank apart—and above scrutiny—as we will discuss later in our book). It is also illustrative of the sensitivities that have existed between the churches of East and West ever since.

Sylvester II, serving from 999 to 1003, was formerly named Gerbert of Aurillac, a native of Auvergne, France. He was a Renaissance man *avant la lettre:* He studied science and mathematics in Spain and was versed in music, literature and philosophy. He is said to have introduced Arabic numerals to the West. The Roman populace thought him a sorcerer, and the English chronicler William of Malmesbury says that Sylvester once conjured up the devil to escape a pursuer. Small wonder he is sometimes considered the prototype for Faust.

Also French was Pope Urban V, who reigned from 1362 to 1370. A Benedictine monk and canon lawyer, Guillaume de Grimoard was the sixth of seven French popes to reign in Avignon, in France. In 1367 he tried to reestablish the papal presence in

POPE LINUS

*Catholics are familiar with, and some are curious about, a line in the Eucharistic Prayer I recited at Mass each Sunday: "We honor Linus, Cletus, Clement, Sixtus . . ." Who in the world were they? Well, they were four of the first seven popes, all now saints, and Linus, seen here, was Peter's successor—the second-ever pope, the original inheritor of St. Peter's throne. How certain can we be about this? Reasonably. Irenaeus wrote in the second century, "The blessed apostles, then, having founded and built up the Church, committed into the hands of Linus the office of the episcopate." And the **Liber Pontificalis,** a medieval book of papal biographies, listed Linus as the second bishop of Rome, after Peter, and continues that Peter ordained two bishops, Linus and Cletus, the latter of whom we will meet on the following page.*

LINVS·I·PP·VOLATERRA

*After two millennia, St. Peter's throne has been occupied by all manner of prelates—
from the holiest of holy men to clearly flawed individuals. Here is
a brief overview, with emphases on popes and papal stories that still resonate today.*

POPE ANACLETUS

With the third pope, Anacletus, or Cletus (for years, his pontificate was erroneously divided into two in narratives, until it was realized that both concerned the same man), the papacy first fell, perhaps, to a Roman. Linus was reported to be well known to Peter and Paul and the disciples, and if that was true, he may have been from the Holy Land. According to most sources, Anacletus was a Roman (the minority view calls him a Greek), and he was pope for a dozen years— maybe 80 to 92, maybe 76 to 88. If the Italian dominance of the pontificate was initiated with Anacletus, so, apparently, was papal activism. Church history says that Anacletus divided Rome into 25 parishes and was proactive in the ordination of new priests. The Church, certainly still under the Roman emperor's boot, was, if not flexing its muscles, at least exercising. Anacletus is buried next to Linus in St. Peter's Basilica, which seems altogether fitting: two early leaders of the Church, hard for us to know but prominent in prayers and also in the continuity that led to the rise and rise of Christianity.

Rome, which popes had avoided for more than 60 years, owing to the ceaseless power struggles on the Italian peninsula. After a stay of almost three years, Urban left Italy on September 5, 1370, despite a warning from the saintly seer Bridget of Sweden that he would not live very long if he returned to Avignon. He arrived September 27. He died December 19. He is remembered in central Europe as the founder of the great universities located in Vienna and Kraków.

France had popes, and so did its rival England— one of them, Adrian IV, born Nicholas Breakspear, who served from 1154 to 1159. He remains unloved in one very Catholic country: His 1155 papal bull, *Laudabiliter,* conferred the overlordship of Ireland on the English king Henry II. The consequences of that concession have caused much pain and suffering through the centuries, and resonate today.

Born Rodrigo de Borja y Doms in Spain, Alexander VI, the Borgia pope whose tenure lasted from 1492 to 1503, has become a signature figure for lust, avarice and nepotism in the Church. His papacy was corrupt from the start, having been achieved by bribe. When chests full of gold were observed in

POPE GREGORY I

Also known as Gregory the Great, he was a monk and a deep-thinker. He became pope on September 3, 590, and was a prolific writer, perhaps more so than any pontiff theretofore; his Dialogues *redefined the religion, and he is known as "the Father of Christian Worship." The moment he died he was canonized, and today he is a saint in the Roman Catholic, Eastern Orthodox and many Lutheran churches, and in the Anglican Communion. He is as well the patron saint of musicians, singers, students and teachers.*

transit from the Borgia palazzo to Cardinal Sforza's on the morning following Rodrigo's election, Roman cynics began to smile. Only in his death did Alexander come to justice. Contemporary chroniclers said he succumbed to poison after dining at the villa of Adriano Cardinal de Corneto; it seems that Alexander accidentally drank from a tainted cup he had intended for his host.

Visiting with these few popes certainly humanizes not only them but also the office they held and the Church itself, and so does a quick look at a few remarkable women who have had an impact upon the papacy—some of whom certainly make us wonder about the current hot-button issue of women being kept from the priesthood. Primary would be Catherine of Siena (1347–1380), who like Francis of Assisi and Joan of Arc was one of those holy agitators thrown up by the Middle Ages to discomfit moribund institutions and societies. A mystic and a stigmatic who was considered a saint by her fellow citizens when still in her teens, she managed

to blend selfless humility and boundless arrogance. She badgered leaders with letters of advice, reserving some of her most impassioned missives for Pope Gregory XI, imploring him to return the papal court to Rome from Avignon, where it had languished. "Come without fear, for God is with you," the dyer's daughter assured the aristocratic pontiff. "Wait not for time because time waits for none. Answer the Holy Ghost." Catherine's exhortations were successful, and Gregory arrived in Rome in 1377.

Olimpia Maidalchini (1594–1657) was a sister-in-law of Pope Innocent X; she selected his cooks—and his cardinals. "She visits the pope every other day and the whole world turns to her," wrote one contemporary. In spite of the power accruing to her influence over Innocent, Olimpia treated him with grisly disregard on his death. She claimed that she could not afford the funeral expenses, and his body lay decaying in the sacristy of St. Peter's until a canon of the basilica agreed to foot the bill. Perhaps Olimpia's resources had slipped her mind. When she died two years later, she left two million scudi in gold.

Josefine Lehnert (1894–1983) was a farmer's daughter from Bavaria. Sister Pascalina (as she was known in religious circles), or La Popessa (as she was known to the irreligious), was housekeeper to Pope Pius XII for 41 years. During that time, stories of Pascalina's power mushroomed. Perhaps the most memorable involved her encounters with the formidable French prelate Cardinal Tisserant. Once, according to Vatican observer Nino Lo Bello, Tisserant arrived in a papal antechamber demanding to talk to the Holy Father, but Pascalina refused him admittance. When Tisserant insisted, Pascalina called for a detail of Swiss Guards to escort him out.

And then there is—maybe; probably not—Pope Joan. An enduring tale during the Middle Ages held that the papacy had been breached by a woman, this "Pope Joan." Joan, the story went, was an Englishwoman who dressed in men's clothing; she became famous for her learning and was elected pope sometime between the middle of the ninth century and the end of the 11th. Her sexual identity was at last betrayed when she went into labor while on horseback. So widespread was the colorful fable that Joan's head appears amid the papal busts in the Cathedral of Siena. The myth was exposed—generously, it might be thought—by a Protestant scholar at the time of the Reformation.

Pope Joan didn't really travel incognito most likely because she didn't really exist. But there were actual people and doings every bit as weird as her story was, and they account for many a colorful chapter in the long history of the papacy. "Let's all dress up as soccer players," a cardinal was heard to remark during the reign of Pius XII. "Then we'll certainly be received [by the Holy Father] right away." Was that subterfuge accomplished? History doesn't tell us. But strange convergences between the secular and non- at the Vatican have been plentiful, and are irresistible to recall. Early accounts of meetings with popes tell of such figures as the six-year-old English prince who would become King Alfred the Great being received by Benedict III in 855, and the Scottish warlord Macbeth by the saintly Leo IX (seen at right) in the 1050s. Recent popes, however, have been open not just to princes and chieftains but also to prison inmates, firefighters and celebrities of various persuasions. (Bob Dylan entertained John Paul II, and so did break-dancers.) A few fun encounters down the ages:

Leo I, on the throne from 440 to 461, met Attila the Hun, no less, near Mantua in 452. As a result of the encounter, Attila, "the Scourge of God," as he became known, left Italy, thus sparing Rome and the Holy See. Leo was not the only prelate to disarm the notorious military leader. The French bishop Lupus of Troyes managed to persuade him to spare the province of Champagne. "I can conquer men," Attila is supposed to have said, "but not the lion and the wolf." *Leo* is Latin for lion; *lupus* is Latin for wolf. Many centuries later—in the 20th, in fact—two popes enjoyed audiences with personages far more peace-minded than Attila, and we recount these if only to show that the leader of the Church can deal with anyone in the world from Attila to . . . well, Clark Gable. Anyone familiar with the mien of Pius XII, whom we will visit in greater depth (and in photographs) later in this chapter, might be fairly amazed to learn that the austere-looking pope, who served from 1939 to 1958, was a movie buff. Yet such was his esteem for Gable that the pope kept another visitor waiting for two hours while he talked with the King of Hollywood. Whether Pius's subsequent caller showed any impatience while he cooled his heels is not recorded, but it is unlikely: He was the much loved Bishop Angelo Giuseppe Roncalli, later Pope John XXIII, whom we will also meet more closely, just a few pages on. If Pius liked moving pictures, Paul VI, whose tenure lasted from 1963 to 1978, was a fan of the written word—particularly the word as written by the English novelist Graham Greene, several of whose books had been banned by the Church, as Greene pointed out to the pope during their audience. Paul was apparently unperturbed and told Greene he earlier had recommended his work to Pius XII. Pius, unknown perhaps to Paul, had not been enthusiastic and told Father John Heenan (later cardinal archbishop of Westminster), "I think this man is in trouble."

POPE LEO IX

The former Bruno von Egisheim und Dagsburg was a forceful reformist pontiff who took the throne in 1049 and held it until his death in 1054. He reinforced priestly celibacy and battled all forms of simony (again, the taking of money in exchange for holy sacraments). He quarreled with and then excommunicated Michael Cerularius, Patriarch of Constantinople, in 1054, thus severing relations between the Roman and Eastern churches. Not such a wise move in the short term, perhaps, but at least the split, which would be called the Great East-West Schism, gave definition to the religion, allowing the orthodox movement to strengthen in the East, while Roman Catholicism could grow in the West. Leo IX, born to the German aristocracy, was not content with his papal purview, and ruled much of central Italy in a secular fashion while fulfilling his religious role in Rome. He is today a saint in the Catholic Church.

Many men have been in trouble, and many others have caused trouble, in the Church hierarchy; there has been skulduggery and there has been violence. The shocking assassination attempt on John Paul II in 1981 was only the latest in a string of assaults that have beset popes through the ages. Ever since Saint Peter was put to death during Nero's persecutions, bishops of Rome have been kidnapped (Silverius, 536–537), strangled (Leo V, 903), suffocated (John X, 914–928), poisoned (John XIV, 983–984, et al.), forcibly deposed (Gregory VI, 1045–1046, et al.) and otherwise disposed of (Benedict XI, 1303–1304, is reported to have died from powdered glass mixed in with his figs). Some other dire doings, not invented by Umberto Eco:

Martin I, who came to the throne in 649, defied the edict that papal elections were not valid unless approved by the Byzantine emperor in Constantinople, and after being consecrated without this sanction, found himself in a peck of trouble. A viceroy arrested the ailing pontiff (he had gout) and forcibly removed him to Constantinople, where he was chained, publicly flogged and exiled to the Crimea. He died from his harsh treatment soon after. Martin is the most recent pope to be revered as a martyr.

The 1517 assassination attempt on Leo X featured clichés familiar in Renaissance conspiracies: family pride, poison and revenge. Leo was being treated for piles when his physician fell ill, and Alfonso Cardinal Petrucci offered a substitute—a pawn of Petrucci's who would poison the ointment being used on the papal disorder—but the modest Leo declined the doctor's attentions. Petrucci was found out, arrested and tortured, and he implicated other cardinals. Magnanimously, Leo let the conspirators go (with huge fines); less generously, he had Petrucci strangled, albeit with a rope of crimson silk.

Pius VI, whose term was from 1775 to 1799, was one of two popes to be abducted from Rome to France by Bonapartist forces (the other was his successor, Pius VII). When he was arrested, age 80 and dying, he refused to remove the papal ring—the Ring of the Fisherman, a symbol of papal sovereignty, which Benedict XVI had to relinquish upon his retirement this year—and asked to be allowed to die in Rome. He was told, according to historian Christopher Hibbert, "People die anywhere." Pius's "anywhere" was Valence, France, where he was imprisoned. French officials called him Citizen Pope.

Again to Paul VI, who during a visit to the Philippines in 1970 was nearly stabbed by a Bolivian. The attack was thwarted by a solidly built cleric. The story grew that the hero was the Italian-born U.S. bishop Paul Marcinkus, whose six-foot-four

stature and athletic reputation had made him a familiar media figure. However, reported Vatican correspondent Peter Hebblethwaite, the attacker had actually been overwhelmed by an English bishop—a mere six feet tall—who was traveling in the papal party.

So there have been bad guys and even bad popes, but it is important to distinguish the latter from antipopes—a term that needs to be understood. In olden days (there haven't been any antipopes since Felix V in the mid-15th century) they were claimants to the throne, when the throne was often disputed and often seemed up for grabs. They were not necessarily bad men, and some are warmly remembered by historians today. For instance: Visitors to the baptistery in Florence are occasionally bewildered to come upon the tomb of an early 15th century pope called John XXIII (whose picture can be seen on page 64). Surely that name belongs to a beloved pontiff of the 20th century, the aforementioned former bishop Angelo Giuseppe Roncalli? Canonically—officially, in Church terms—it does. The John XXIII enshrined in Florence, not

BPK, BERLIN/OESTERREICHISCHE NATIONALBIBLIOTHEK/ART RESOURCE, NY

POPE URBAN II

The pontiffs we isolate for closer examination were not all saints or heroes, and Urban II is remembered by history as neither—but he was hugely influential. In 1095 he put his Church and all of Western Christendom squarely in opposition to Islam by inciting the First Crusade. The ramifications in his time were great, and the repercussions even today are obvious. For 200 years, beginning in the late 11th century, there was a continuous series of holy wars between Christians and Muslims, based in Europe and in the Holy Land—eight major Crusades during the period—and something

ALBUM/ART RESOURCE, NY

necessarily an evil man when alive (though he was a serial womanizer), is an antipope, one of a series of bishops of Rome whose papal tenure is not accepted as valid by the Holy See. But again: *Antipope* does not mean Antichrist. Two antipopes are revered as saints, though—yes—others led less edifying lives.

The third-century Greek theologian Hippolytus is considered the first antipope. His rival—the man deemed official—was Callistus I, pope from 217 to 222, whose liberal attitude toward celibacy and abortion Hippolytus abhorred, an interesting reversal of the relative positions of theologians and the papacy today, and certainly not a philosophical or political precedent that was cited at the recent conclave. Since both Hippolytus and Callistus suffered heroic deaths for the cause of Christianity, they have presumably found harmony in being enshrined in the Church's catalogue of saints.

Anacletus II, an antipope from 1130 to 1138, was born Pietro Pierleoni and was descended from an illustrious Jewish banking family, many of whom converted to Christianity on Easter Sunday in 1030 and one of whom became a canonically accepted pope, Gregory VI (1045–1046). Anacletus's claim was opposed by two emperors—the Holy Roman and the Byzantine—but the key opposition came from the Middle Ages' great scourge of unorthodoxy Bernard of Clairvaux, who alluded to Pierleoni's Jewish ancestry as a reason for denying him the papal chair.

We have mentioned the earlier John XXIII, a claimant from 1410 to 1415: He was the Neapolitan Baldassare Cossa, one of the last antipopes, and flourished during the Great Western Schism (1378–1417), a period of such confusion that during Cossa's "reign" there were three claimants to the papal throne. We will learn a bit more about all this in our next chapter, but for now: After Cossa was deposed by the Council of Constance, the universally acknowledged Pope Martin V appointed him cardinal bishop of Tusculum.

So much and so many who were less than exemplary! Where is the sunshine in the papacy?

Let us turn, finally, to the saints and blesseds who, after all, are decreed by popes.

As can be seen on the list that accompanies this chapter, a great many popes themselves have been canonized as saints, and it is anticipated that John Paul II will join them one day—probably one day in the not distant future. He was an important figure in this question of sainthood when he walked in our earthly realm, as he made canonizations and beatifications a hallmark of his papacy. He created hundreds of saints and 1,786 "blesseds" (the most elevated waiting category for candidate saints)—astonishing statistics, considering that only 302

like that is never forgotten. Urban II was born Odo of Lagery in France and, as a prelate, became a favorite of Pope Gregory VII, whose reforms (a strengthening of the papacy, an affirmation of priestly celibacy) he would continue to champion during his own regime, which began in 1088. He was approached in 1095 by Byzantine emperor Alexius I Comnenus, who asked for support against the Muslims in Anatolia (today Turkey). Urban was receptive, to say the least. He convened a council that year at Clermont in his native country, and several hundred bishops, archbishops, abbots and noblemen attended. He

gave an effective sermon, that much is certain. There are five versions of his speech, each written after the fact by men who may have been at the council or may have gone on a Crusade. Their accounts generally agree that Urban spoke of the violence in Europe, the need for peace, a willingness to help the Greeks, the righteousness of an armed pilgrimage and blessings for those who joined the fight. Beyond that, the transcriptions vary, and political motives are clearly at play. One version has Urban calling for Christians to destroy "that vile race . . . Christ commands it." That source also has him promising "immediate

remission of sins" for all who die in battle against the "pagans." Another—only one—has the famous scene in which the crowd responds to his call for blood by shouting "God wills it!" and so we might assume pro-Crusade propaganda rather than journalism. Nonetheless, it was Urban who sent them off, and the goal soon became not just assisting the Byzantine emperor against the Muslim Turks but the retaking of Jerusalem, which was accomplished on July 15, 1099 (opposite, the conquest of Jerusalem in an illuminated manuscript page). Urban died two weeks later, before word of the event reached Rome.

saints and just 2,000-odd blesseds were named in the previous 400 years. From John Paul's roster, a few stand out, three because of the celebrity—or notoriety—that has accrued to their names, others because they were victims of, or heroes in the face of, the tyrannies or cruel inequities that have haunted modern times.

Juan Diego (1474–1548) is the champion of a famous tradition in Guadalupe, Mexico, in which the Virgin Mary is said to have appeared to the Aztec (or Chichimee) layman and to have left her image miraculously imprinted on his cloak as evidence for doubters. Diego's beatification in 1990 helped John Paul achieve two goals: to promote devotion to Mary (he was the most Marian pope ever) and also to demonstrate—by honoring different ethnic traditions—that the Church is catholic as well as Catholic.

Padre Pio (1887–1968) was born Francesco Forgione, and even while he lived he was the object of a flourishing cult. In 1918 he was said to have received the stigmata—that is, wounds identical to those of Christ on the cross. Other stories told of his power of healing and of his ability to be in two places at once. But some Church authorities were unimpressed, and for several years before World War II the Vatican forbade him to say Mass publicly or hear confessions. Nevertheless, the young Father Karol Wojtyla visited Padre Pio in 1947 (after the ban had been lifted); according to one report, the friar told his guest—the future John Paul II—that he would hold "the highest post in the Church." Padre Pio was beatified in 1999 and canonized in 2002, John Paul his patron in both cases.

Titus Brandsma (1881–1942) was a Dutch Carmelite who in 1935 was dubbed by the Nazis "the dangerous little friar." Why? He had stated bluntly that Catholic papers could not in good conscience publish Nazi propaganda, an affront for which the Germans sent him to Dachau following their occupation of the Netherlands. "They who want to win the world for Christ must have the courage to come into conflict with it," said Brandsma. This uncomfortable conviction cost him

POPE PAUL III

A modern Western sensibility does not so much recoil at the biography of Paul III—who stood at the intersection of so many off-shooting roads in the Church's history—as ask, bewildered: What do we make of this guy? He was besieged by events not of his own making, he was proactive in other areas in unfortunate ways: He cheapened the Church by baldly practicing nepotism at the Vatican. And yet, finally, he held his Church together in the face of the Protestant Reformation. Hero? Villain? Take your pick. Or a little of both?

He was born Alessandro Farnese in 1468 and was a cardinal in the Church when Rome was sacked in 1527; he became pontiff seven years later. It was a real question at that time whether the Church would survive. Martin Luther (whose picture Paul is looking at, opposite) had marched off with his Protestants, and all sorts of suborders were forming in the shadows— Jesuits, Theatines, Barnabites and the like. (The Jesuits would of course endure, and Pope Francis is one.) As pope, Paul III seemed at least as concerned with building his family's wealth and power as he was with figuring out the schism at hand. He had a lot of folks in the house to take care of, as he had fathered four illegitimate children before his election as pope. He created one of his sons as the duke of Parma and an early action was to decree his two teenage grandsons cardinals. He was a patron of the arts, and during his tenure Michelangelo rendered the "Last Judgment" in the Sistine Chapel and was commissioned to paint both the "Crucifixion of St. Peter" and the "Conversion of St. Paul" and to oversee the completion of St. Peter's Basilica. Nicolaus Copernicus dedicated On the Revolutions of the Heavenly Spheres *to Pope Paul III. But then, Paul, according to some sources, okayed the enslavement of Muslims (other sources say he was against slavery generally). But then again, even in the face of Luther's determination, he kept the Catholic Church that exists today moving forward. He is, historically, the embodiment of so much that has been good and bad in Rome—and he is scarcely to be believed by a modern Christian.*

his life. He was killed by lethal injection on July 16, 1942, and beatified as a martyr of the faith in 1985.

Edith Stein (1891–1942) was a Carmelite nun who converted to Catholicism in 1922; she was known as Sister Teresa Benedicta of the Cross. The daughter of a Jewish family in Breslau, Germany, she was sent by her order to Holland in 1938. She was arrested by the Gestapo and deported to Auschwitz, where she soon perished in the gas chamber. Her beatification (in 1987) and canonization (in 1998) were resented by some Jewish critics who claimed it was her Jewish origins, not her Catholic faith, that led to her death. One of her nephews, however, told *Time* magazine that her recognition by Rome was "a spiritual monument to all those killed by the Nazis."

Josemaría Escrivá de Balaguer (1902–1975) was the founder of Opus Dei (and in a way the founder of all that *Da Vinci Code* zaniness). It is useful to know that his institution was intended, foremost, to induce laypeople to integrate spirituality with their everyday lives. Although Escrivá and his organization have been criticized by some Catholics, who compare their methods to those of such as the late Reverend Sun Myung Moon, John Paul's admiration was always staunch and demonstrative. In 1982 he made the institute a personal prelature, meaning that it was answerable not to local bishops but directly to the Supreme Pontiff, and in 1992 he raised Escrivá to the ranks of the blessed; a decade later, JP II made Escrivá a saint.

Mother Teresa (1910–1997) was born Agnes Gonxhe Bojaxhiu and founded the Missionaries of Charity, which today has more than 4,500 sisters working in 133 countries, providing everything from a cup of soup to hospice services for the poorest of the poor. She won the 1979 Nobel Peace Prize for her extraordinary efforts, and was beatified as Blessed Mother Teresa of Calcutta in 2003, only a few years after her death—the speediest to reach that stature until her own patron, John Paul II, was put on an even faster track to sainthood by Benedict XVI. When Gallup took a poll to find the Most Admired People of the 20th Century, humble Teresa finished first.

All of these many men and women, from Peter to Teresa, are players in the story of Rome and of the Church. On the following pages, we look more closely at a few important pontiffs of recent years, and then we look back at Benedict XVI's term and forward to that of Francis.

The papacy has, clearly, been through tumultuous times and times of calm. It is in a difficult period just now, there is no question about that. With the election of Cardinal Bergoglio, it hopes it is emerging.

THE POPES, FROM PETER TO THE PRESENT

The history is nearly two millennia long and has often been amended and will be amended again. The Roman Curia's official roster of popes, now called the *Annuario Pontificio*, has undergone near constant modification down the decades—dates, birthplaces, even names being changed, added or subtracted. As Pope Francis begins his pontificate, here is the list of 266 men and their years of tenure.

1. Saint Peter (32–67)
2. Saint Linus (67–76)
3. Saint Anacletus (Cletus) (76–88)
4. Saint Clement I (88–97)
5. Saint Evaristus (97–105)
6. Saint Alexander I (105–115)
7. Saint Sixtus I (115–125)
8. Saint Telesphorus (125–136)
9. Saint Hyginus (136–140)
10. Saint Pius I (140–155)
11. Saint Anicetus (155–166)
12. Saint Soter (166–175)
13. Saint Eleutherius (175–189)
14. Saint Victor I (189–199)
15. Saint Zephyrinus (199–217)
16. Saint Callistus I (217–222)
    Callistus and the following three popes were opposed by Saint Hippolytus (217–236), antipope
17. Saint Urban I (222–230)
18. Saint Pontian (230–235)
19. Saint Anterus (235–236)
20. Saint Fabian (236–250)
21. Saint Cornelius (251–253)
    Opposed by Novatian (251), antipope
22. Saint Lucius I (253–254)
23. Saint Stephen I (254–257)
24. Saint Sixtus II (257–258)
25. Saint Dionysius (260–268)
26. Saint Felix I (269–274)
27. Saint Eutychian (275–283)
28. Saint Caius (283–296)
29. Saint Marcellinus (296–304)
30. Saint Marcellus I (308–309)

POPE PIUS XII

In what Pope John Paul II once called "this difficult century"—the 20th—three popes in particular were buffeted by modern events, and made their mark: Pius XII, John XXIII and John Paul himself. Issues on the table for these three, whom we will visit on the next 12 pages, included the threats of fascism, Nazism and communism; an increasingly secular and progressive world; an onrushing globalization of all

matters. Everything involved the Church at a near or far remove, from war and peace to civil rights movements to apartheid to feminism to the pill to sexual abuse. At century's end, the 1.2 billion strong Catholic faithful (the world's largest religion), were left with a reformed Church but also new skepticisms about their leaders and priests. They and the world at large had weathered the worst storms of tyranny, but there were other, sometimes unexpected

problems and debates.

First we look at the ever controversial Pope Pius XII. Counterclockwise from top left, the Italian cardinal Eugenio Maria Giuseppe Giovanni Pacelli sits in the back of an open car during a parade in 1935, and then there are two photographs from his first year as pope in 1939: In June, three months after his installment, Pius has his ring kissed by a general during an audience for Spanish troops at the Vatican, and

in December Pius leaves the Presidential Palace in Berlin. This last is a particularly ominous picture, considering the twists and turns of the Pius story: He was elected pope just before World War II broke out, and there is little question that he tried to be diplomatic in dealing with the war's increasing horrors—an approach that cast a shadow over his papacy. He took as his motto Opus justitiae pax, "The work of justice [shall be] peace," but whether

he sacrificed human justice to keep some sort of peace—whether, to put it clearly, he was too soft on fascism and was not proactive as Hitler's regime exterminated millions of Jews—remains the question.

Some brief background: Before he was elected pope, Cardinal Pacelli was not only the Vatican's secretary of the Department of the Congregation for Extraordinary Affairs but also secretary of state, and earlier had served for 12 years as the

HULTON-DEUTSCH/CORBIS

papal nuncio to Germany and Bavaria—so he had been tied up in European (specifically German) affairs since even before the armistice that ended World War I. History tells us that the reapportionments and other harsh conditions imposed upon Germany after that war left a breeding ground for radical movements such as ultra-nationalistic Nazism, but be that as it may: In this postwar period Pacelli was, if not altogether passive, diplomatic (as might be expected of a papal envoy). His assignment, simply put, was to serve the Vatican. The concordat of 1933 was seen in Rome as a way to preserve and protect Catholicism in Germany, where the Church was one of Hitler's enemies (despite the fact that Hitler was born a Catholic). That's what Pacelli was concerned with. There is little evidence that Pacelli, before the advent of World War II, was concerned as well with the persecution of other faiths, and some historians have discerned anti-Semitism in his comments and actions (or inactions) as a younger man.

There is no doubt that he was opposed to Hitler, someone he considered, as quoted by historian Joseph Bottum, "an untrustworthy scoundrel and fundamentally wicked person." On April 28, 1935, Pacelli gave a speech to a quarter million pilgrims in Lourdes, France, in which he baldly said that Nazis were "in reality only miserable plagiarists who dress up old errors with new tinsel. It does not make any difference whether they flock to the banners of social revolution, whether they are guided by a false conception of the world and of life, or whether they are possessed by the superstition of a race and blood cult." The following year, Pacelli met with U.S. President Franklin Roosevelt and certainly stressed again that the Vatican was not neutral vis-à-vis the Nazis; on another occasion he told the American ambassador to the Court of St. James (U.K.), Joseph Kennedy, that rapprochement with the Third Reich should be "out of the question." (Kennedy, an appeaser himself —it would cost him his job—would have disagreed.) The American consul to Berlin, A.W. Klieforth, wrote that Cardinal Pacelli "did not believe Hitler capable of moderation, and . . . fully supported the German bishops in their anti-Nazi stand."

But on the other side of the coin: In this period several governments were dealing with what they considered "Jewish

PIX INC. (2)

BETTMANN/CORBIS

issues"—Hungary as well as Germany was promulgating anti-Semitic laws, for instance—and Pacelli was heard to refer to Jews "whose lips curse [Jesus Christ] and whose hearts reject Him even today." When Kristallnacht, the Nazis' 1938 pogrom against German Jews, stunned many awake, the Vatican, of which Pacelli was secretary of state, refrained from condemning the violence. If Europe was headed for a conflict as the 1930s neared their end, so was this man.

And then, on March 2, 1939—his 63rd birthday—he was made pope.

The famous retort regarding papal power or influence in military affairs belongs to Joseph Stalin, who, when asked about the value of the Vatican's support to Russia's enemies, answered, "How many divisions does the pope have?" But in fact, moral authority does carry weight, as we will see when we discuss John Paul II's opposition to communism, and the larger question is whether a pope chooses to exercise that authority.

As we have seen: By the time Pacelli became Pius in March of 1939, he already had deep experience in the European situation that would come to define him, and also had a track record. The war came to his

very doorstep (opposite, top, at the Vatican in 1940; at bottom, his damaged Vatican apartment after a bombing raid of Rome in 1943). Pius remained anti-Nazi and, as is mentioned elsewhere in these pages, made arrangements for the papacy to continue without him should he be taken by agents of the Third Reich.

But did he do enough to support or aid the persecuted Jews? That has always been the big question, and the arguments on both sides are vehement to this day. Pius's supporters say that his perceived reticence was strategic; that he felt the Vatican could help more by behaving in a surreptitious fashion; that when some of the allied nations were refusing Jewish immigrants, the Vatican was printing hundreds of false identifications that would allow Jews to pose as Christians and flee Europe; and that—most of all— when Germany invaded Italy in 1943 and propped up Mussolini, Pius ordered an effort to shelter thousands of Jews in convents and monasteries throughout the country, even in the halls of the Vatican itself.

His critics allege that the Church stayed unforgivably silent during the Holocaust: It did not exercise its moral authority in the greatest moral

issue of the age, and if it wasn't willing to do that, what if anything did it stand for?

After the war, Pius, as any pope might, urged leniency toward the defeated Axis countries—a stance that would only serve, over time, to bolster the condemnatory position. His papacy was far from done. A modern pope, he took often to the airwaves, and all came to know him in the postwar period as a fierce anticommunist, not that this had much effect on the persecution of priests in Eastern European countries now under communist rule.

He looked inward and instituted reforms of the Church. He was never inactive, and as he approached his 80th birthday in March of 1956, Roman schoolchildren (above) were happily among the thousands in St. Peter's Square waiting for their Holy Father to appear at the apostolic window, accept their good wishes and offer his blessing. Pius XII died in 1958 and was succeeded by Pope John XXIII, whom we will meet on the pages immediately following.

He was declared Venerable by Pope Benedict XVI in December 2009, and he may be canonized one day. But if his soul rests in peace, his reputation will never be resolved to the satisfaction of all.

POPE JOHN XXIII

His smile was beatific, and his personality inspired. But John was not content to be passively charismatic. He wanted to change the Church, and the world with it. He began a dialogue with the Soviet regime, and he told Jewish visitors, "I am Joseph, your brother." His encyclical on government's responsibility to address social as well as political problems, Mater et Magistra ("Mother and Teacher"), was considered so liberal by some conservative Catholics that one was prompted to respond: "Mater, sì! Magistra, no!" Whether his papacy was in reaction to that of Pius XII or simply in relief when contrasted with it does not matter. What does: The Church hadn't seen anything like John XXIII in a long while, if ever, and despite the attractiveness of

John Paul II and that pope's accomplishments, it hasn't seen anything like him—or his landmark achievement, Vatican II—since.

He was born Angelo Giuseppe Roncalli, the third child of 13, in a small rural village, Sotto il Monte, in the Lombardy region of Italy in 1881. His parents were sharecroppers, and his heritage in relative poverty would be yet one more thing standing in contrast to that of Pius XII, once Roncalli was made pope. He is seen at right, in the center, while studying for the priesthood in Rome in 1901; he would be ordained in 1904. He was secretary to the bishop of Bergamo for a period, lectured in a seminary and then served in the Italian army. During World War I, he returned to the front, first as a hospital orderly, then as a military chaplain. (Below: He is seated,

TULLIO FARABOLA/STR/AP

center, with the hairline already receding toward the golden dome that would be one of his cherished hallmarks.) After his discharge from the army in 1918, his career in the Church began in earnest. He was a star but not a supernova, with some notable, and curious, achievements on the résumé. In 1921, Pope Benedict XV made him the Italian president of the Society for the Propagation of the Faith, a sign that he was large on the Vatican's radar. In 1925 Pius XI named him the apostolic visitor to Bulgaria, and, like Pius XI and XII,

LUIGI FELICI/AP

Roncalli would become well versed in—and a player in—the dramatic happenings in Europe in this period. In 1935 Roncalli was made apostolic delegate to Turkey and Greece, and saw the advancing persecutions firsthand. He went to work. Before and during the war, he acted openly with petitions and interventions and also clandestinely. He aided the movement of Jewish Slovakian children and Jewish refugees from Turkey to safe harbors; he helped to keep Jews from being deported to concentration camps. What fueled him, apparently, was a basic humanity; he once looked back and explained, "We are conscious today that many, many centuries of blindness have cloaked our eyes so that we can no longer see the beauty of Thy chosen people nor recognize in their faces the features of our privileged brethren. We realize that the mark of Cain stands upon our foreheads. Across the centuries our brother Abel has lain in blood which we drew, or shed tears we caused by forgetting Thy love. Forgive us for the curse we falsely attached to their name as Jews. Forgive us for crucifying Thee a second time in their flesh. For we know what we did."

The snowstorm in the picture below was in Paris in 1952, and the following year Roncalli became a cardinal. Just five years later he succeeded Pius XII as pope. He was nearly 77, and it was thought that he would behave as a caretaker for a short term, then quietly exit the scene. Boy, did John XXIII have surprises in store for the Vatican.

AGIP-RUE DES ARCHIVES/GRANGER

He perceived a changed world and an unchanged Church. He called the Second Vatican Council in 1962 and encouraged reformers—the young men who would become future popes John Paul II and Benedict XVI among them—to speak freely, and advance their hopes and dreams. Particularly in fast-moving postwar societies like that in the United States, the freshness of Vatican II was inspiring. Here was a Church we could embrace. And as the council began, John XXIII proved the world's best salesman: a warm, kindly grandfather type who, with a wink of the eye, knew exactly

AP

HANK WALKER

PAUL SCHUTZER

what was going on and enjoyed a good joke. You can see it in the pictures on the opposite page, clockwise from top left: with U.S. First Lady Jackie Kennedy (a Catholic) in 1962; with England's Queen Elizabeth (an Anglican) the previous year; and borne to the opening of the Ecumenical Council in St. Peter's in '62. Below: Under the Bernini Canopy in St. Peter's, the council gets under way on November 1 with more than 2,600 archbishops and bishops gathered to pay John homage during the opening ceremony, then to get to work. John XXIII would die the following year; the council would continue until 1965, passing historic reforms, attempting to make the Church more of a service to its people. One man's awesome legacy.

CARLO BAVAGNOLI

153. Victor II (1055–1057)
154. Stephen IX (1057–1058)
155. Nicholas II (1058–1061)
    Opposed by Benedict X (1058), antipope
156. Alexander II (1061–1073)
    Opposed by Honorius II (1061–1064), antipope
157. Saint Gregory VII (1073–1085)
    Gregory and the following two popes were opposed by Clement III (1080–1100), antipope
158. Blessed Victor III (1086–1087)
159. Blessed Urban II (1088–1099)
160. Paschal II (1099–1118)
    Opposed by Theodoric (1100– 1101), Aleric (1101) and Sylvester IV (1105–1111), antipopes
161. Gelasius II (1118–1119)
    Opposed by Gregory VIII (1118), antipope
162. Callistus II (1119–1124)
163. Honorius II (1124–1130)
    Opposed by Celestine II (1124), antipope
164. Innocent II (1130–1143)
    Opposed by Anacletus II (1130–1138) and Victor IV (1138), antipopes
165. Celestine II (1143–1144)
166. Lucius II (1144–1145)
167. Blessed Eugene III (1145–1153)
168. Anastasius IV (1153–1154)
169. Adrian IV (1154–1159)
170. Alexander III (1159–1181)
    Opposed by Victor IV (1159–1164), Paschal III (1164–1168), Callistus III (1168–1177) and Innocent III (1179–1180), antipopes
171. Lucius III (1181–1185)
172. Urban III (1185–1187)
173. Gregory VIII (1187)
174. Clement III (1187–1191)
175. Celestine III (1191–1198)
176. Innocent III (1198–1216)
177. Honorius III (1216–1227)
178. Gregory IX (1227–1241)
179. Celestine IV (1241)
180. Innocent IV (1243–1254)

POPE JOHN PAUL II

By any accounting, he was one of the giant figures of the 20th century, a man at the center of several storms, a man who seemed, truly, somehow elevated above his fellows (which of course is a claim he would never have made). He was born Karol Wojtyla in 1920 in Wadowice, 30 miles from Kraków (and only 15 miles from Auschwitz) in Poland. His mother, Emilia, sensed he was destined for greatness. Helena Szczepanska, a neighbor who used to babysit the young Karol, who was nicknamed Lolek, once recalled, "His mother used to yell up to us to say, 'You will see what a great man will grow from this baby.' We all used to laugh at her and say she had a loving heart but could not predict the future. But everyone fussed over him as if he was a prince, so you never can tell."

Wadowice at the time was a town of 8,000 Catholics and 2,000 Jews, among them burghers, farmers, professionals and merchants. Located in the Carpathian foothills, it derived its character from the mountains and the wondrous medieval and Renaissance city Kraków. This modern Poland was brand new. The nation had been obliterated in the late 18th century, its parts divided among Austria, Prussia and Russia. For more than a hundred years, restoration of sovereignty had been the Polish dream, but it wasn't until 1918, when Woodrow Wilson's postwar Fourteen Points included "independence for Poland," that the dream was realized.

All of this—the Polish Catholicism, the Jewish neighbors, the surrounding mountains and rivers, the romance and traditions of Kraków, that city's hallowed places of learning, the remembered pain of a vanished nation, the glory of its resurrection and the sweet taste of freedom—all of this would

VIVIANE RIVIERE/SIPA

inform who and what Karol Wojtyla would become. Lolek grew up devout, smart, poetic and thoroughly ecumenical: Many of his friends on the soccer pitch were Jewish.

By the time of Lolek's graduation from high school (above) he had been acting for four years in the joint boys and girls' theater group, the Wadowice Theater Circle. But the cloth would call him away from the stage, and after the Nazi tanks rolled across Poland in the 1930s, he found his future at an underground seminary in Kraków. He knew that friends, particularly Jewish ones, were disappearing. "I was spared much of the immense and horrible drama of the Second World War," he wrote of his days as a seminarian. "I could have been arrested any day, at home, at the stone quarry [where he worked], in the plant, taken away to a concentration camp. Sometimes I would ask myself:

so many young people of my own age are losing their lives, why not me? Today I know that it was not mere chance."

Destined for true greatness as his mother had predicted, he would rise in the Church after the war, would star at Vatican II and would be elected pope in 1978 after John Paul I died only 33 days into his term. In the other photos on these pages, clockwise from right, in 1979 John Paul II and Mother Teresa visit her mission in Calcutta, India; he tours the former Nazi concentration camp at Auschwitz-Birkenau, where some of his friends and many other Jewish Poles died; he poses before the Statue of Liberty, also in 1979. He was from the get-go an on-the-go pontiff, spreading the word, spreading himself thin. It all looked happy and almost easy for a short time. And then everything got much more serious.

GILLES PERESS/MAGNUM

RAGHU RAI/MAGNUM

BRUNO BARBEY/MAGNUM

On May 13, 1981, while riding through St. Peter's Square and greeting the characteristically large and rapturous gathering, John Paul was shot twice by Mehmet Ali Agca and critically injured (right). He recovered, and now he was truly larger than life—even more beloved, more influential. Working behind the scenes with other world leaders—activist union chief Lech Walesa (in the photograph at bottom, receiving communion from the pope in their mutual homeland, Poland, in 1987); Margaret Thatcher, prime minister of Great Britain; Ronald Reagan, President of the United States—he helped bring about the fall of communism. In the aftermath, he was one of the world's great ambassadors, welcomed nearly everywhere. In the photograph at center, John Paul reviews some rare books at the Vatican with, of all people, Soviet president Mikhail Gorbachev and Gorbachev's wife, Raisa. It can be said: John Paul II was his Church's greatest evangelist since Paul of Tarsus.

His was the second longest pontificate in history, ending only with his death in 2005. It is commonly accepted that he was frail and less effective in his final years, but he understood always that the institution he was leading and the world in which he was living faced severe trials. His faith sustained him. When he addressed these 26 newly ordained priests, who are lying face down during a presbyterial solemn ceremony in St. Peter's Basilica on May 2, 2004, the 83-year-old Holy Father told them to stay true to their calling. "You are becoming priests," he said, "in an age in which, even here in Rome, strong cultural tendencies seem to want to cause people to forget God."

He had lived through it all—death camps, atheistic communism, an assassination attempt, the waning influence of his Church in Europe, the sexual abuse scandals—but he never would, nor ever could, forget God.

EPA/CORBIS

RUDI FREY

GIANNI GIANSANTI/SYGMA/CORBIS

The Others Who Resigned

Here we see in a 16th-century painting the coronation in 1294 of Pope Celestine V, who would be canonized in 1313 as Saint Celestine. Once a hermit and for much of his life intensely ascetic, he attracted many followers—they were later called Celestines—but was a reluctant pontiff. He was already in his eighties when he assumed the throne, and he quite quickly realized that the administrative duties at the Vatican were not only beyond his undeveloped talents but were distracting him from his spiritual quest. He told the cardinals of his concerns and resigned within a matter of months: "We, Celestine, Pope V, moved by legitimate reasons, that is to say for the sake of humility, of a better life and an unspotted conscience, of weakness of body and of want of knowledge, the malignity of the people and personal infirmity, to recover the tranquility and consolation of our former life, do freely and voluntarily resign the pontificate." Celestine's successor, Boniface VIII, reacting to a growing furor that the unprecedentedly willful resignation had been unlawful, had Celestine kept under wraps at Fumone Castle, where he died not long thereafter in 1296. Dante condemned Celestine for quitting, placing "him who made, through cowardice, the great refusal" at the very gates of the Inferno. Benedict XVI, however, saw a kinfellow, and in 2010 traveled for a second time to Sulmona in Italy's Abruzzo region to venerate Saint Celestine's relics.

AS WE HAVE SEEN IN THE PRE-vious three chapters, the story of the papacy and the men who have held it has been long and twisting. (This, it should be acknowledged, would be expected with any institution or government so old, especially one that has persevered through so many periods of social tumult.) As for the 266 official popes, the vast majority of whom you will not meet in these pages: The line of Church leaders from Saint Peter to the present has not always proceeded neatly, as we have also seen, and certainly not all of the men who have sat upon the throne have seemed infalli-ble—not, at least, in human terms.

While we are on this point: Even some of the assumptions about popes have changed through the centuries. Let us indeed consider for a moment the particularly famous Church dogma of infalli-bility, which maintains that the sitting pontiff, as Christ's vicar via the original promise to Peter, can-not possibly be wrong when delineating "a doctrine concerning faith or morals to be held by the whole Church." Not a scintilla of argument is to be coun-tenanced on such matters.

But, while popes have long been credited with ethical and spiritual superiority, papal infallibil-ity was not specifically declared—certainly never so emphatically—until the First Vatican Council in 1869 and 1870. (The Vatican would stress that popes prior to the conclave had been spiritually infallible too—grandfathered in, as it were.) So the fact is that new rules, descriptions and inter-pretations of scripture have been written through the years. To cite another example: Many people assume that, since the beginnings of Christianity, or certainly since the earliest schisms that brought about the freestanding Church, there has been an edict banning women priests. Not quite so. It wasn't until 494 that Pope Gelasius I saw fit to con-demn the ordination of women. The argument that Christ had declared His intentions by choosing all male disciples, while it now has a long history, was not always the accepted wisdom.

As for the tradition that popes do not retire: It is only that—a tradition. It's not any kind of law; it has long simply been an assumption, a given. In fact, popes do step down, and can, and historically have even been persuaded to. It is certain that four sim-ply resigned—gave it up—prior to Benedict XVI,

This year, the news that a pope can step down took many by surprise.
After all, it hadn't happened in nearly 600 years. But it *had* happened.

To understand the case of Gregory XII (opposite), the last pope before Benedict XVI to resign, one needs to understand the Western Schism of 1378 through 1417 (also called the Papal Schism or the Great Schism, though the East-West Schism of 1054 is sometimes called the Great Schism too). The turmoil within the Church in the late 14th century amounted to political, nationalistic war without the weaponry; all official popes in this period—Urban VI, Boniface IX, Innocent VII and then Gregory—were opposed during their terms by at least one antipope, as factions in Avignon and Pisa saw the Church in Rome as vulnerable (or rightly theirs). At certain points, there were riots in Rome to keep the papacy there. Angelo Cardinal Correr, who would become Gregory XII, agreed during his time as a candidate that to end the schism he would, if elected pope, resign his title if the Avignonese claimant Benedict XIII pledged to do the same—and then a unified church could choose a new man. Once enthroned in 1406, however, Gregory stayed seated, fending off for a time antipopes Benedict XIII, Alexander V and John XXIII. In the engraving on this page, antipope John XXIII is entering Constance, Germany, where an ecumenical convocation of the warring factions is beginning that would lead, during sessions from 1414 to 1418, to the resignation of Gregory and the renunciation of claims by two of his great rivals, Benedict and Alexander. The eventual winner would be the Church and also the newly elected Pope Martin V, an Italian like Gregory but one who had supported the antipopes Alexander and John, and who was now named the spiritual leader of all Christendom.

and more may have done so.

As with many issues within the church, this is complicated. Some popes in days of yore were said to have resigned but there's not enough evidence, and others were involuntarily deposed; the Church does not count these as having been valid resignations. (As an aside, while headline writers sometimes use the word *abdicate*, the Church does not—it's always *resign*. And *quit* is nigh on blasphemy.) In the third century, according to some sources, Pope Pontian resigned, but we can't be sure. It's the same with Pope Marcellinus in the early fourth century. Some stories have Liberius resigning and some have him clinging to the papacy in exile. John X may have resigned, but he may have been deposed; in any event, he apparently died in prison even before the next pope, Leo VI, was elected. Where are the resignations in the exceedingly strange saga of John XII, Leo VIII and Benedict V? Let's try to get this straight: John was deposed in 963, Leo was established as antipope, John reclaimed the throne, John died, Benedict was elected, Benedict was apparently deposed, Leo reascended. Get it? Got it? Good.

In sorting that one out, the Vatican has decided that Benedict V's resignation was not coerced—or not egregiously so—and that Leo's succession was legitimate (meaning, among other things, that Leo has the distinction of having been both a real pope and an antipope).

Another Benedict—the ninth—also resigned. (With the resignation of Benedict XVI in 2013, that papal name certainly carries a legacy of foreshortened tenures.) Benedict IX's final résumé is as fascinating as any: He became pope in 1032, was deposed briefly in 1044, came back for a month in 1045 and then resigned. He enjoyed a third term in 1047 and 1048 and then resigned again. Moreover, it turned out he had been bribed to resign the first time (bribed, incidentally, by the man who would become Pope Gregory VI, who himself would be deposed). So Benedict IX is the only man to have been pope thrice, and the only man to have sold the title.

While a couple of those historical resignations seem irrefutable, there have been two other cases of resignation before Benedict XVI's that are considered, by the Church, "canonical"—those of Celestine V after just 161 days in office in the 13th century, and Gregory XII after nearly nine years on the throne in the 15th century. After Gregory resigned on July 4, 1415, the Church would see a run of 598 years with popes dying in office until Benedict XVI stepped down.

But even in this period, there were intriguing episodes that warrant a footnote, two of which occurred in the past century. Some historians have written that Pius XII authored a letter stating that if the Nazis ever arrested him, his resignation should be taken as de facto and the papacy should continue with a new man. And it is known that John Paul II, in his frail later years, put it in writing that if he should become medically incapacitated, he ought to be replaced.

Pope Benedict XVI

In the modern age and with the problems facing the modern Church—some of these problems certainly of the Church's own making—being pope has become one of the world's toughest jobs. In his eighties, Benedict was overwhelmed by his duties. ✝

IN OUR TIMES, NEW POPES are always greeted with great joy and optimism by the flock. Here is a man (no matter which man he is) who has dedicated his life to God and to serving the message of Jesus Christ. Here, now, he comes to lead us. The throngs in St. Peter's Square and beyond may hope or dream of great things to be accomplished, but even that doesn't matter at the moment. They behold a man, a holy man, and they congratulate him on his ascension to the throne and wish him nothing but the best. As they raise their voice in hosanna, they are certain that the cardinals have chosen wisely. This is the man who was meant to be next. This is the Vicar of Christ.

It was that way when Joseph Alois Ratzinger of Marktl am Inn, Germany, was elected pope in 2005, despite a life and career and age that might have given pause. Now, after nearly eight years and the first resignation of a pope since 1415, and with the Church confronted with all manner of scandal (sex abuse, financial corruption at the Vatican Bank, the VatiLeaks pilfered-documents case), the sympathetic faithful are saying that, well, Ratzinger tried. He was simply overwhelmed. The less charitable are saying he failed, and we might have seen it coming.

It seems clear, now, that he was too old for the job. The Vatican and the Curia are always reactive and oftentimes overthink things. When Paul VI was followed by John Paul I in 1978, and then that pope lived only 33 days after his coronation, the thinking was, among other things: We need a young, fit pope. John Paul II was hale and hearty indeed, even surviving an assassin's bullet, but when his papacy extended to more than 26 years, the last of which were seen as unsuccessful, the thinking became: Enough of that; we need a caretaker pope. And so Ratzinger—conservative in doctrine, a talented theologian, a JP II loyalist—was elected at age 78, the oldest new pontiff since Clement XII in 1730. Clement lasted another decade before he died, but Benedict could not persevere that long before his retirement.

On these next several pages, the man's journey, as he heads into his prayerful and hopefully peaceful retirement from the papacy.

World War II greatly informed the youths and young adulthoods of both Karol Wojtyla, who would grow to become Pope John Paul II, and Joseph Ratzinger, who would be Benedict XVI. As we now know, Wojtyla saw Jewish friends in his Polish town disappear (Auschwitz, again, was just down the road), and he studied for the priesthood at an underground seminary in Kraków. Ratzinger was six years old in 1933, when the Nazis came to power and, by the time he too entered seminary in 1939, had come to share his devout parents' anti-Nazi views. Yes, in 1941 he became a member of the Hitler Youth—he was compelled to join—and in 1943 he was, as was any able-bodied German man, drafted into the military. That's precisely when the picture on this page was taken: during his first year with an antiaircraft unit. He was allowed in this period to still attend school in Munich three days a week. In 1945, assigned to set tank traps in Hungary, he deserted, was captured by American forces, spent a brief time as a prisoner and then, after the war, went on with his career in the Church. On the opposite page, top left: Brothers Georg (left) and Joseph Ratzinger are ordained to the priesthood along with 42 other young men on June 29, 1951. When Pope Benedict XVI announced his resignation in 2013, it fell to Georg to speak for his brother—his health, his motives—and all these years later, people came to know the Ratzinger boys quite a bit better. At top right, in 1978, West German cardinal Ratzinger, archbishop

of Munich and Freising, is grasped warmly by the new pope, John Paul II, during the solemn inauguration of John Paul's ministry as universal pastor of the Church. Ratzinger would become one of JP II's most influential and trusted aides. At bottom: The cardinal in 1993 in his office at the Vatican, doing what he enjoys most—and some say does best—reading and thinking. Even his detractors concede that he has long been a brilliant and important theologian, and it was his thinking, even before he authored seminal works including Introduction to Christianity *in 1968 and* Dogma and Revelation *in 1973, that first brought him to the attention of higher-ups in the Church.*

Ratzinger was recruited to be the archbishop of Cologne's expert assistant at John XXIII's history-making Second Vatican Council in Rome from 1962 to 1965. He was seen at the time as a young lion, an energetic reformist. Another who fit that description at Vatican II was the auxiliary bishop of Kraków, Wojtyla, who was one of the council fathers and took those reins firmly in his grasp, writing forcefully and persuasively about how Catholicism might answer the challenges of modernity—how Christianity could supply a "soul" to an increasingly soulless world. The two men already knew one another, and their mutual admiration would do nothing but increase through the years.

As a loyal right-hand man of John Paul II, one who had helped the increasingly frail pope cope with his infirmities in old age, and prefect of the Congregation for the Doctrine of the Faith, the man most responsible for interpreting and preserving Catholic doctrine, Cardinal Ratzinger was one of the favorites to be elected pope in the spring of 2005—which of course meant he would not be elected, since the College of Cardinals seemed, historically, to have a penchant for surprise, as with the choices of both popes named John Paul (not to mention Francis). And yet, on April 19, the second day of the conclave, Ratzinger won the approval of more than two-thirds of his fellows. Five days later he celebrated his papal inauguration Mass, took the name Benedict XVI and greeted those of his followers who had gathered to celebrate him in St. Peter's Square (above). Right: On May 2, the one-month anniversary of John Paul II's death, the new pope prays for his late friend at the legendary man's tomb beneath St. Peter's Basilica. There is no testimony that, at this point in time, Benedict is wondering whether he can measure up. But so many of the problems that beset John Paul in his later years, particularly a tsunami of new revelations in the church-wide sexual abuse scandal, quickly fall to Benedict. At what point the pope realized it might all be too much for him, or that his diminishing health would necessitate an end, has been speculated upon but is finally left for the historians to ascertain.

In the first years of his papacy, Benedict was up and about and even traveled, though there was no way he would ever rival the peripatetic John Paul who, in evangelistic and often ecumenical outreach during the salad days of his papacy, logged more miles around the globe than all 263 previous pontiffs combined. Above, Benedict kisses the Stone of Unction in the Church of the Holy Sepulchre on the final day of a five-day sojourn in Israel and the Palestinian territories in 2009. His open hand to other religions, particularly to Islam, would finally be judged as reluctant or altogether wanting. Left: Back home in 2010, at what is often called the pope's "summer residence," Castel Gondolfo, just south of Rome, it's movie night. Rather than Mel Gibson's Passion epic, Benedict has chosen Under the Roman Sky. This film stars James Cromwell as Pius XII, and details that pope's brave efforts to save the lives of Jewish Romans after the city has been occupied by the Nazis. Some historians have less lofty views of Pius's actions during World War II, as we have seen in the previous chapter, but Benedict is firmly in Pius's camp, and in fact did his part to smooth the road to sainthood by declaring Pius "Venerable" in 2009.

The road to sainthood begins with local bishops conducting a preliminary investigation of their candidate, after which the candidate is presented to the Vatican Congregation for the Causes of Saints. Once the nominee is accepted for consideration, he or she is named a Servant of God. Next, the candidate's writings are looked at closely and possible miracles attributable to the deceased's posthumous intervention are examined. If the Vatican determines that the candidate is a person of "heroic virtue," he or she is declared Venerable. Then, once a miracle has been officially sanctioned, the candidate is called Blessed, and he or she is beatified. And then, finally: Sainthood. Some of these stages can be passed over in extraordinary cases, and, here, John Paul II's beatification ceremony is presided over by Pope Benedict XVI on May 1, 2011. A million and a half people crowd toward St. Peter's, the largest crowd in Rome since John Paul's funeral six years earlier. The casket in which the late pope had been interred has been brought up for public veneration, and Benedict prays before it. The casket is then placed in the Chapel of St. Sebastian after the ceremony, and Benedict returns to far more burdensome duties. He faces less than two years' time remaining in his tenure, though no one—not even he, certainly—could predict such an eventuality at this moment.

In his later months as pope, Benedict rarely travels, and if he isn't found at the Vatican itself, he is probably at Castel Gandolfo, a good place to think things over while resting on a bench beside the lake or casting bread upon the water for the fish (opposite). Finally he has made his consequential—monumental—decision, and on February 11, 2013, he slips the news into his remarks (left) during a consistory for the canonization of the martyrs of Otranto: some 800 southern Italian Christians who were killed by the Ottomans in 1480 for refusing to convert to Islam. Many of the attending cardinals miss entirely what Benedict is telling them about himself, so close has he kept his secret to this point. But soon it becomes clear: He will retire at month's end. Officials at the Vatican come to life and realize that deft planning might result in the election of a new pope during Lent, perhaps even a coronation before Holy Week and a glorious Easter for a Church recently beset by nothing but bad news. The wheels start turning; Benedict himself waives the normal waiting period after the death of a pope before voting can begin; the 115 cardinals who will take part in the conclave begin making their way to Rome. Benedict himself goes about his final duties while on St. Peter's throne, assisted at every turn by aides, as he has been for a while now. Below: He leads Ash Wednesday Mass at the Vatican on February 13 at the beginning of the 40-day Lenten season. During the conclave, Benedict spends his time at Castel Gandolfo; he will be there for the next two months, too, as the refurbishment of his new home in Rome is completed.

OR/CPP/POLARIS

ALESSANDRO BIANCHI/REUTERS

February 28 is as highly emotional a day as it is unusual, and leaves the Church with an altogether novel situation. Above: It has been decided that Benedict will leave Vatican City by helicopter, and therefore dramatic photography of the crowd in the gallery on the roof of St. Peter's Basilica, bidding a tearful farewell to their leader, is disseminated around the world. The trip to Castel Gandolfo is less than 15 miles and takes no time at all. At some point Benedict, who has been positioned as a postmodern, connected pope during his pontificate, issues his last tweet (right) while officially still the Vicar of Christ, urging his followers to keep Jesus as a guiding force. At the summer residence, he appears before his flock for the last time in his papal vestments (opposite). The crowd cheers. On this day he tells the faithful that he is beginning the final stage of his life as "simply a pilgrim." In Castel Gandolfo, at eight p.m. local time, his eight-year tenure is over. Benedict will be pope emeritus for the rest of his life, but has taken an extraordinary oath of obedience to his successor, and has indicated that, by and large, he will stay out of Vatican matters and spend much of his time in prayer and contemplation. Nevertheless, there exists a certain awkwardness.

PETER MACDIARMID/GETTY

ALESSIA GIULIANI/CPP/POLARIS

The Church is left with its traditional "empty chair" that has always followed the death of a pope, but there is no funeral, no mourning. If anything, Benedict's departure while still alive allows commentators—and presumably the cardinals who are gathering—to focus more forthrightly on all the many problems the Church faces. The cardinals can be a little more clear-eyed and less sentimental about Benedict's pontificate and legacy (which we will briefly examine on the pages immediately following) when they break bread at meals in early March, and then enter the top-secret conclave in the Sistine Chapel on March 12. On that morning, in fact, Angelo Cardinal Sodano's homily for his brethren while celebrating a final public Mass prior to the conclave alludes, however gently, to the troubles, and calls for an arm-in-arm front at a time of disarray. The dean of the College of Cardinals says from the pulpit: "Saint Paul teaches that each of us must work to build up the unity of the Church. All of us are therefore called to cooperate with the pastors, in particular with the successor of Peter, to obtain that unity of the Holy Church." Sodano, who served both John Paul II and Benedict XVI as secretary of state during the last two decades, does pay tribute to the former pope, citing the "luminous pontificate [of the] beloved and venerated pontiff Benedict XVI," but the overarching message of his sermon, the last instruction delivered before the doors are closed, is unmistakable: Now is not the time for schism or vendetta, now is the time to coalesce, clearly define what we stand for and move forward as one Church.

STÉPHANE COMPOINT

direct response to sex-abuse allegations in that country, and yet in the spring of 2012, when Benedict was visiting there, he delivered a homily not of contrition, but rather one that denounced a local reformist priest and called for Catholics to adhere to "the radicalism of obedience." Those words, in the face of the legal, secular, human facts of sexual abuse, seemed the last thing needed. So did, earlier in his pontificate,

some of his words on Islam. Several times he bent over backwards to be cordial or even welcoming to Muslims, and that was heartening, since the religious divide was such an immediately critical world issue. But on September 12, 2006, Benedict delivered what would be called the Regensburg Lecture at a university in Germany where he had once been a professor of theology. Considered now one of the most significant papal

arguments on world affairs since John Paul II appeared at the United Nations in 1995, the speech included a quotation from the 14th-century Byzantine emperor Manuel II Palaeologus that was unambiguously critical of Muhammad and Islam. Street protests followed in the Middle East, and editorials around the world questioned the pope's real feelings about ecumenism. Benedict had scant success in his tenure

On this page we see Benedict walking away with the aid of his cane after delivering his last message from the Castel Gandolfo window on February 28, and on the opposite page we see a member of the Vatican Swiss Guard closing the main door of the papal residence there, signaling clearly the end of Benedict's pontificate. He resides at Gandolfo still today while work continues at the Mater Ecclesiae in the Vatican Gardens (above), which will be his retirement residence once it is readied. The renovation on what was recently a nuns' convent began discreetly in November, indicating that some few knew of Benedict's intention to resign. He will be happy there: The building has a chapel, a roof terrace with views of St. Peter's Basilica and access to the gardens, where Benedict has enjoyed walking in the afternoons. That will be the peaceful setting for his twilight.

He was born on Holy Saturday, the day before Easter, in 1927 to a family of modest means from Lower Bavaria, and grew up in an environment that he, an accomplished pianist, once described as "Mozartean." The comfort and spiritual nourishment he found at home was quickly in conflict with what he saw of the real world, as he witnessed Nazis beating the local parish priest before Mass. He grew, as we have said, to be a man of deep thought, and then he rose in

the Church, and became pope: All of that is well known, delineated in these pages and elsewhere. What of his legacy? It is thought that his papacy, as opposed to the man himself, will not be judged kindly by history. In 2005 there was hope—and indication—that there might be a freshening inside the Vatican, but this didn't happen. As to the sexual abuse scandal, Benedict quickly met with victims in the United States and the United Kingdom, apologizing to them and stressing that he and his Church felt "shame and humiliation." As recently as 2011 he told bishops to be proactive in rooting out misbehavior by any clerics. But then: There was much evidence of bishops enabling abusive priests by looking the other way or covering up, and these bishops were not dismissed by Benedict. There was no move to institute a level of accountability at the Vatican. The news continued to pour forth from around the globe, and Rome appeared increasingly callous. Americans were stunned that Roger Mahony, the former Los Angeles archbishop who in recent months has been linked to the sheltering of abusive priests, was not banned from the conclave to elect Benedict's successor. In the U.S. and throughout Western Europe, Catholics continued to leave the Church in droves. In Austria, for instance, it has been asserted that 150,000 deserted their religion in

L'OSSERVATORE ROMANO/AP

at building bridges with the Christian Orthodoxies, which have long been at odds with Rome, or with Judaism—not that he expended capital in these areas, as his predecessor had. On another issue facing the modern Church: In the autumn of 2012 the Vatican fired an American priest who had participated in the ordination ceremony of a woman, despite evidence that Catholics in the U.S., Europe and almost everywhere supported not only admitting female priests but allowing male priests to marry.

Certainly, this can be seen, particularly in a sophisticated theologian such as Benedict, as an adherence to principles. But it did little to stanch the Church's bleeding. Benedict and his fellow cardinals seemed okay with this. They steadfastly refused to deal even with issues that appeared simple to address on nontheological grounds. The Vatican Bank has long been corrupt, a hotbed of intrigue, with rumors of financial misfeasance, money laundering, mob connections and even murders, but Benedict did little to clean up the mess, and even as the conclave began in the Sistine Chapel on March 12, there was debate among the voters as to whether the next pope should wade in—or should just let matters lie, and protect as sacrosanct the secrecy of all Vatican doings. The so-called VatiLeaks scandal, begun by an Italian television news show in January 2012, seemed of more concern to the Curia: How do we quell all these allegations of the blackmailing of homosexual clergy in Rome in these financial and other scandals? It was a mess, it was a hornet's nest, and it is no wonder at all that any 85-year-old person might have felt it quite beyond his earthly powers to deal with it. Benedict resigned, and all of the above was left to his successor.

Pope Francis

✝ *The College of Cardinals went "to the end of the earth" to find the right man to lead the Church out of its darkness. The world prays that this very different kind of pontiff can show the way.*

IT WAS MARCH 13, THE SECond day of the conclave in the Sistine Chapel to elect a new pope, and the votes seemed to be swinging his way. This had happened once before to Jorge Mario Cardinal Bergoglio, who back in 2005 had drawn surprisingly strong support from his clerical brethren. He reportedly said at the time that he didn't wish to be pope. That was fine, because in any event he finished second to Cardinal Ratzinger. Now, however, the tide was inexorably turning. The votes were being counted after the fifth ballot, and Bergoglio was going to be chosen. His closest friend among the 114 other cardinals in the room, Cláudio Hummes, the former archbishop of São Paulo, Brazil, was sitting by his side. If the soon-to-be pope was not allowed to display undue emotion, Hummes could. He hugged Bergoglio, then kissed him. "Don't forget the poor," he said.

"And those words entered here," Pope Francis remembered later, indicating his head and his heart. "The poor, the poor. And then, right away, in relation to the poor, I thought of Francis of Assisi."

Any learned Christian might well think first of Assisi—if not Christ—when considering the poor. The Italian Catholic friar who in the early 13th century founded the order that has become the Franciscans had forsaken his considerable store of worldly goods to live humbly in poverty, advocating for and supporting the neediest among us.

Indeed, much about the new pope seems to have been modeled on the example of Assisi. "Humble" has been used to describe him over and over again, and it is doubtful that he could ever forget the poor, coming, like Cardinal Hummes, from a Latin country that is rich in Catholics and rich in want. The course that will be charted for the Church by the former Cardinal Bergoglio is yet unformed, but he was forthright and inspirational in his first steps as Pope Francis: Focus on the poor. Be charitable. Be honest. Stay humble. Reach out beyond Catholics. Lead, from the outset, by deed.

PIERO OLIOSI/POLARIS

Those first days in Rome, between the revelation on March 13—*Habemus Papam Franciscum*—and the coronation on March 19, were filled with moments large and small, many of which are pictured in the pages to follow: the pope asking his people to bless him before he bestows a blessing in return, the pope on the bus, the pope paying his own tab at the hotel, the pope sticking with his comfortable shoes and eschewing the red slippers, the pope reaching out to a score and more of children or infants, and them reaching back for him (or crying their eyes out, undone by the hubbub), the moving Mass at the smaller Church of St. Anna, the moving sermon on a beautiful day during his installation Mass in immense St. Peter's Square. Meantime Jorge Mario Bergoglio's story was found and told: Yes, he's Argentinean, but Italian, too; yes, he's 76, and has only one lung; it's true he cooks his own meals; he is in fact a Jesuit; he certainly was in Argentina during the Dirty War, and whether he did enough to oppose the junta is for others to judge.

Finally: He is ready to serve his Church, and to serve the poor. He said so. Eight years ago, he didn't feel ready. Today, he does.

Above: One of Giotto's series of frescoes in the Basilica of St. Francis in Assisi, high on a hill in Italy's Umbria region, where the young man remade his life, shows Francis talking with the birds. (Francis is the patron saint of animals, among other things. A side note: Many of the frescoes were badly damaged, and 10 people were killed, in back-to-back 1997 earthquakes.) When Cardinal Bergoglio chose Francis as his papal name, many thought he might be honoring the 16th-century missionary Francis Xavier, cofounder of the Society of Jesus (the Jesuits, of which Pope Francis is one). But the new pontiff subsequently explained that his inspiration was indeed Assisi, who after forsaking his high-living ways became, as Francis put it, a self-made "poor man, a simple man, as we would like a poor church, for the poor." Opposite: As a boy in Buenos Aires.

At right is the circa 1943 register in the Pedro Cervino school in Flores, a neighborhood of Buenos Aires, showing that young Bergoglio is making satisfactory progress. (What else would you expect? He was a good boy, too.) Far right: In this family photo, are (top row, left to right) Alberto Horacio Bergoglio, his brother Jorge Mario, their siblings Oscar Adrian and Marta Regina and (bottom row) sister Maria Elena, mother Regina Maria Sivori and father Mario José. (Only Maria Elena and Jorge Mario are still alive.) The dad was a railway worker in Buenos Aires who had moved the family from Portacomaro, near Turin in Italy's Asti province, to get away from the fascist regime of Benito Mussolini. (In the photograph at bottom, the future pope, second from left, visits the village back in northern Italy where his father was born.) Jorge Mario was born in 1936 and was a smart boy with solid prospects. He received a chemical technician's diploma in secondary school, but the priesthood called, and, in his early twenties, Bergoglio began studying at the archdiocesan seminary Inmaculada Concepción in Buenos Aires's Villa Devoto. He was a thoroughly normal young man, with a deep devotion to his soccer team, San Lorenzo de Almagro, and a love of music and dancing, particularly if the tune was an upbeat tango. He is also a fan of the traditional South American milonga. These last résumé items would serve him well when, as a cleric, he developed a reputation as a man of the people—tango dancers and fellow soccer fans could relate to Father Bergoglio. When he was 21 years old, he had a setback: He developed pneumonia and lost most of one lung to infection. This of course

became part of the news when Pope Francis was elected: The cardinals have chosen a not-quite-trim 76-year-old with one lung. When Francis was seen to stumble slightly on his second day in office, the suspicion strengthened: They've elected another caretaker—placeholder— pope. They don't want another

reign like John Paul II's. But in those few days between election and installation, the people in the pews got to know Francis for the first time, and many came to hope that their new pontiff, who seemed sharp as a tack from the pulpit and when dealing with the press, might be with them for a good long while.

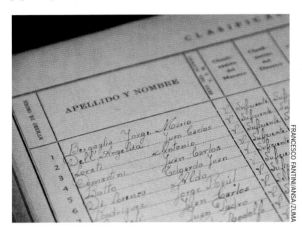

FRANCESCO FANTINI/ANSA/ZUMA

ANSA/ZUMA

ANDREA PAVESI/OLYCOM/SIPA

The Jesuits have a deserved reputation for intellectual development, and it takes dedication and time to become one. After three years at the seminary Bergoglio had made his decision, and he entered the Society of Jesus in March of 1958. He would not be ordained to the priesthood until December of 1969. Which is not to say he was always in the library: He taught in college as his own education progressed. As a priest (left, during services in Buenos Aires), he continued for a time as a professor of theology, then, finally having completed his spiritual requirements, took his perpetual vows as a Jesuit in 1973; he was named provincial superior of the Society of Jesus of Argentina that year, and would serve in this post throughout the decade. What an awful decade that would prove to be. When the military junta seized power in March of 1976, Father Bergoglio was 39 years old. The next seven years were times of terror in Argentina, as perhaps 30,000 unionists, journalists, students and priests—anyone thought to be left-wing or even mildly subversive—were rounded up and killed, raped or "disappeared." All was havoc. These many years later, there is clear concern in the hierarchy of Argentina's Catholic Church that it did not do enough to protect victims during the dictatorship; an apology issued by the bishops last October said as much. Pope Francis has, in recent days, been accused of having sat on the sidelines; specifically, that he was complicit in the capture of, or did little to help free, two kidnapped Jesuit priests who endured a brutal detention before finally being released. One of the priests criticized Bergoglio's handling of the incident before he died; the other, still living, said he and Pope Francis have made their peace. Cardinal Bergoglio, in one interview and additional testimony during a court case, said that he did try to work behind the scenes during the Dirty War. Much like the debates about Pope Pius XII's behavior during World War II, this will never be resolved. Below: The Mothers of the Plaza de Mayo protest the lack of action on missing members of their families in October 1982.

Clockwise from top left: On February 21, 2001, Jorge Mario Bergoglio is made a cardinal by Pope John Paul II in the consistory in St. Peter's Square at the Vatican; back home, the cardinal passes in front of the Basilica of Our Lady of Luján, less than 50 miles from Buenos Aires; on May 25, 2006, he is alongside Cristina Fernández de Kirchner during a Mass at the Metropolitan Cathedral in the Argentine capital. Bergoglio had first been made archbishop of Buenos Aires in 1998, and for 15 years he was a dominant force in the country and, at regular intervals, a thorn in Kirchner's side. The relationship with the Argentinean president began when Bergoglio clashed with Mrs. Kirchner's predecessor, her husband, Néstor Kirchner, who died in 2010. At one point, during a Mass, Bergoglio sermonized about hypocritical politicians as the Kirchners sat in the pews. More consequently, Bergoglio's conservative views on social issues (which will certainly be an issue during his papacy) were at odds with the more liberal views held by the Kirchners, as well as many of Bergoglio's countrymen. Pope Francis is a fundamentalist

on current Catholic doctrines regarding abortion, the ordination of women, same-sex marriage and adoption of children by gay couples, the last of which he has called a form of discrimination against children. In 2010, in a battle over the legalization of gay marriage and adoption by same-sex couples in Argentina (a measure that passed, with Mrs. Kirchner's support), he said such practices were "a war against God" and "a maneuver by the devil." Kirchner called his rhetoric "medieval." She once joked that it was unfortunate she couldn't run for pope, because she would enjoy giving Bergoglio a run for the job. Now, of course, everything is different. Or is it? Kirchner's missive of congratulations to her fellow Argentine was a terse three sentences long. But she did follow this up quickly with a visit to the Vatican and a sit-down with her old foe, and afterward pronounced him "calm, confident and at peace. Tranquil." She also said, perhaps tweaking a bit: "I could also say that he is occupied and concerned about the immense task not only to govern Vatican City State, but to change things that he knows need to change."

83

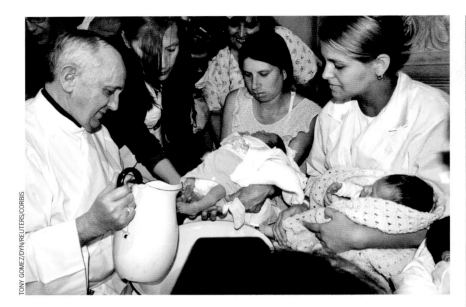

TONY GOMEZ/DYN/REUTERS/CORBIS

ENRIQUE MARCARIAN/REUTERS

EMILIANO LASALVIA/LATINCONTENT/GETTY

FILIPPO FIORINI/DEMOTIX/CORBIS

Long before he became Pope Francis, Father and then Cardinal Bergoglio—to all, "Padre Jorge"—had a reputation back home as a man of deep humility, a man in Francis of Assisi's image if not of his Franciscan order. At left, top to bottom, three photographs from Buenos Aires: On Holy Thursday, March 24, 2005, at the Sarda maternity hospital, he washes an infant's feet in the Catholic ritual; the Virgen de Caacupé chapel in the Barracas neighborhood, where

Bergoglio would minister and say Mass; on May 25, 2008, he engages in conversation on the A-line subway prior to the celebration of the traditional Te Deum Mass at Metropolitan Cathedral. He telegraphed his desire for the Church to reach out to the people and to take risks in this outreach before he was pope. "We have to avoid the spiritual sickness of a self-referential church," Bergoglio told the Italian newspaper La Stampa, referring to evangelism but certainly implying that the to-the-barricades, circle-the-wagons attitudes of recent years would no longer do. "It's true that when you get out into the street, as happens to every man and woman, there can be accidents. However, if the Church remains closed in on itself, self-referential, it gets old . . . I have no doubts about preferring the former." Above: In Buenos Aires on February 13, 2013, for his last Ash Wednesday service as cardinal. He would shortly fly to Rome—and his surprising fate.

On the opposite page: Inside the conclave in the Sistine Chapel on March 12, 2013. There are 115 voters in this extraordinary room, each of whom has taken an oath of secrecy. Truth be told, the ominous hushed tones and implied horsetrading that always attend the conclave, held as it is beneath Michelangelo's fantastic frescoes depicting the beginning and end of the world, are unfortunate this year, as they only reinforce the image of the Church as stuck in the past, stuck—even—in the Middle Ages. The cardinals don't seem to care, but maybe the Vatican's handlers do, because there exists this singular picture, showing orderly proceedings—not any demonstrative, knives-out free-for-all. Not only has the chapel been prepared but so have affairs in the anterooms, where papal vestments in three sizes await whichever-sized pope may be next. (Please note the several shoe boxes on the bottom of the rack.) The victor, once chosen, will be properly garbed before emerging on the balcony of St. Peter's Basilica to greet the faithful below.

The conclave begins on Tuesday with the thought that there are two factions organized for battle—the old-school, pro-Curia group; and progressives, including cardinals from the United States who have been battered by the recent scandals and seek real change. The bookies (and do not bet that bookies don't handle action on such things as a papal election) seem to think that the anti-change wing is backing Odilo Cardinal Scherer of Brazil

(thereby, you get your nod to the Church's significance in the New World while making sure you've got a Curia insider on the throne) and the reformers are supporting Angelo Cardinal Scola of Milan (an Italian, true, but one forceful enough to shake up the Curia). Neither candidacy gains steam during the first few rounds of voting, and by the second day Bergoglio, who has many friends and much respect among those gathered, and who certainly entered the game with his own backers, has emerged as a fine compromise—perhaps even, dare everyone hope, a unifier. The stoves (left) stand ready to burn each round of ballots; smoke will exit from chimneys on the roof, telling pilgrims gathered in the plaza whatever is the latest news. Chemical combustion products are added to control the color—black (for: no pope yet) or white (for: Habemus papam!).

The Vatican doesn't disclose how many rounds of voting are taken to elect a new pope, but as we know only too well: VatiLeaks, even from inside the Sistine Chapel, do exist. It is now believed Bergoglio gained his required two-thirds majority on the fifth ballot. On Wednesday the 13th, the white smokes flutters on the breeze (left). The cheer goes up in Rome, and within moments the tweet from the @Pontifex account alerts the world: a truly bizarre melding of medieval and postmodern methods of communication, and somehow so perfect for the Roman Catholic Church in the 21st century.

Now everyone is on pins and needles for more than an hour: Who is it going to be?

Cardinal Bergoglio was well known to most of his colleagues, but still: You can't figure what you're going to get when you make a man the pope, the father, the "full, supreme, and universal power over the whole Church." The cardinals didn't know if Jorge had been transformed, but they found out quickly enough. It is traditional for a newly elected pontiff to sit magisterially in a chair in the Sistine Chapel while his old friends come up, one by one, to greet him, pledge obedience and kiss his hand, while the folks outside cool their heels. That just wasn't working for Pope Francis, who stood and smiled and accepted congratulations for a bit and then, realizing there were thousands waiting in the rain and that he would hobnob plenty with these other guys in the weeks, months and years to come, asked politely, "Is it okay if I see you afterward? Maybe we should go to the balcony first, because I don't want to keep the people waiting." Everyone agreed this would be a good thing. What else could they do? If there was any grinding of teeth, it went unheard—or at least unreported.

When he appears at the window (opposite), even after the announcement of his papal name seconds earlier, there is still a scrambling for understanding in the plaza and many places around the world. It is nothing like when the familiar and expected Cardinal Ratzinger was elected, but quite like when Cardinal Wojtyla was, and the murmuring started: "What? A Polish pope?" This time it is: "An Argentine? Which one?"

In Argentina, they know immediately, and at the Metropolitan Cathedral in Buenos Aires, where Cardinal Bergoglio has presided at so many Masses, an elderly woman in the congregation is transported by the news (above). From the balcony, Francis asks for the prayers of "all men and women of goodwill," and he gets them. Around the world Catholics celebrate and in Spanish-speaking countries they dance in the streets. Even in India, where Catholics constitute only 1 percent of the vast population, a talented sand artist sends best wishes from a beach on the Bay of Bengal (right).

There would be so many grace notes that would start people buzzing as they grasped for an understanding of Francis. Chief among them, at the outset, there is the blessing from the balcony (below). There always is one: the pope blessing his flock. But this was so very different. "I would like to say a prayer," Francis said, and everyone bowed their heads. But this wasn't yet for them. He first prayed for Benedict XVI, and he went on a little in prelude, asking all the gathered and those listening to take "a journey of brotherhood in love, of mutual trust. Let us always pray for one another." He said, "And now I would like to give the blessing, but first I want to ask you a favor. Before the bishop blesses the people, I ask that you would pray to the Lord

to bless me—the prayer of the people for their bishop. Let us say this prayer—your prayer for me—in silence." He bowed deeply in supplication. The cardinals on either side of him hardly knew what to do. The clamor below subsided. The silence was a thing of beauty. It was perhaps the most peaceful moment the Church had realized in several years.

In the days following that first appearance, Francis steps lively, and continues to make not an errant footfall vis-à-vis his fast-developing public image. Opposite, top: The cardinal has been staying at the Domus Internationalis Paulus VI residence during the conclave, but now he is checking out because, as pope, he has other digs in town at the Vatican. He pays the bill himself. Middle: On the same day, traveling in Rome on official business, he eschews the papal car service and clambers aboard the cardinals' bus to travel with his friends. (Playing a Where's Francis? version of Where's Waldo?, can you guess which cap is the pope's?) Bottom: The fashionable Benedict XVI would recoil to see Francis still wearing his old shoes during an audience in the Paul VI hall at the Vatican with members of the world's media. It is March 16, and these hounds have been nipping at these heels for two days about the Dirty War stories out of Argentina. But Francis is serene (even as the Vatican press office is denouncing the dogs as having an anti-Catholic agenda). In his dealings with reporters before and after his installation, he is introspective (he tells the Francis of Assisi story) and resolutely charming.

And then he does it again. He tells these ink-stained wretches that he realizes many of them are not Catholic, not Christian, not even God-fearing. That's okay; that's fine. Nevertheless, he would like to offer them a blessing—and then he asks if he might do so, in silence. There is no objection.

ODED BALILTY/AP

FRANCO ORIGLIA/GETTY

PAUL HANNA/REUTERS

CLAUDIO PERI/EPA/LANDOV

Top left: Dawn is yet to arrive on Tuesday, March 19, as a group of nuns make their way through a tunnel leading to St. Peter's Square to attend the inauguration of Pope Francis at the basilica. Nuns are nuns, and by and large they are very nice, but they have to make sure they beat out the speedier, *younger women (left) for a good viewing spot on the plaza. As many as a million pilgrims and dignitaries will be crowding into Rome and as many as 150,000 into the square: everyone from U.S. Vice President Joe Biden to the ecumenical patriarch of Constantinople—the first head of the Orthodox Church*

to attend a papal inauguration since Pope Leo IX caused all that trouble 959 years ago (please see page 45). For the Catholics in the massive congregation, the communion hosts are being prepared and then—glory be!—everyone is rewarded with a sunny late-winter's day in Vatican City. If Francis has developed a signature move since being elected pope, it is to stretch his hand to bless a child (above). In doing so, he is clearly every bit as earnest as John Paul II was when he did the same, thousands of times, during his papacy. This is an important gesture in the moment and in and of itself, but, while not wanting to read too much into this, it seems to represent with this new man a realization that the Church's future, whatever that future may be, does not rest with the older men who are awaiting him closer to the altar, but with the people—the people in the streets and in the many churches, thousands of whom have come to celebrate with him this day. Francis opens his arms to them all this day, inviting those of other churches and those without any church to join in building not only a better place for themselves, but to reach down to the poor and help pull them up. One interpretation of his homily: Together we are stronger. Another: We're all in this together.

It is a day of grand gestures, grand but meaningful words and, in many places—Rome and Buenos Aires chief among them—great joy. At right is an aerial view of St. Peter's Basilica at the beginning of the installation Mass. At this moment in Argentina, where the sun hasn't yet risen, the Metropolitan Cathedral in the capital city has been full for some time and the overflow crowd watches the service on big screens in the public square (below). On the opposite page, clockwise from top left: The pallium, an ecclesiastical vestment of the Church that denotes authority granted by the Holy See, is fitted on the pope; the papal miter is placed on his head; the Fisherman's Ring is placed on his finger by Angelo Sodano, dean of the College of Cardinals; the pope celebrates Mass. In his sermon the pope stresses, "We must not be afraid of goodness or even tenderness," and in developing this theme he sketches a world that, surely, seems an idyll to many. It is a world, Francis says, worth working for. There would be, he implies, rewards in the effort itself, which effort would include "protecting people, showing loving concern for each and every person, especially children, the elderly, those in need, who are often the last we think about. It means caring for one another in our families: Husbands and wives first protect one another, and then, as parents, they care for their children, and children themselves, in time, protect their parents. It means building sincere friendships in which we protect one another in trust, respect and goodness. In the end, everything has been entrusted to our protection, and all of us are responsible for it." Where such words will lead from here for Francis will be fascinating to see, and it would be fascinating to know just what he was thinking when, as we see on our book's final page, he gazed upon a statue of Mary and the Christ child during his inaugural Mass and realized at what extraordinary point his journey had already delivered him.

MATTEO LOSITO/ITALIAN POLICE/AP

MARTIN ZABALA/XINHUA NEWS AGENCY/EYEVINE/REDUX

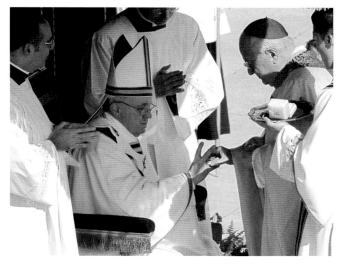